"Finally, here is a book that will not make men feel guilty."
Gary Chapman, author, *The Five Love Languages*

"For several years after retiring as a player in the NFL, I 'kept my helmet on', as my wife, Kim, would say. I only saw what I wanted to see and only heard what I wanted to hear about all that she was dealing with as the mother of our seven kids. Finally, I took the helmet off and learned how to really hear and see her. Had I only had this book ten years ago, we could have saved countless disagreements and discussions! It's a must for husbands who long to raise the communication and intimacy levels in their marriage."
Mike Singletary, NFL Hall of Fame Linebacker

"Whether you've been married a few days or 50 years, *Date Your Wife* is well worth the read. Justin Buzzard shows us the first step to loving your wife isn't to try harder—it's to be empowered by the gospel. *Date Your Wife* gives you biblical advice and practical tips that will transform your marriage."
Jim Daly, President, Focus on the Family

"Finally, here is a book to put in a man's hands that doesn't tell him ten things to do to meet his wife's needs. Instead, *Date Your Wife* gives men a whole new paradigm for marriage: a paradigm of grace, freeing men to approach life and their wife in a whole new way. Once men understand this, everything changes."
Paul David Tripp, President, Paul Tripp Ministries; author, *What Did You Expect? Redeeming the Realities of Marriage*

"This book is for every man who wants a lifelong romance with his wife. Surely that is God's good will. It's why we fully expect God's blessing to be on this book. *Date Your Wife* could be how your romance is renewed for keeps."
Ray and Jani Ortlund, Renewal Ministries

"I want every man I know to read this book. *Date Your Wife* has the power to emancipate men and liberate marriages."
Mark Batterson, Lead Pastor, National Community Church, Washington, DC; author, *Wild Goose Chase* and *Soulprint*

"In this book, Justin has done wives a great service. After being pursued by a husband who's promised to love them, many wives have found that their husbands are now busy pursuing other things—from the NFL to corporate business plans—and that his interests really lie elsewhere. Justin offers the practical help and encouragement that men need to live out the depth of the vows they've made. He does all of this in the milieu of God's grace to us through Jesus Christ. I'm so thankful for Justin and how the Lord will use this book in many lives!"

> **Elyse Fitzpatrick,** counselor; speaker; author, *Because He Loves Me* and *Comforts from the Cross*

"Don't you dare think *Date Your Wife* is a 'been there, done that' book. It's revealing, eye opening, and inspiring. It's fresh. I am certain *Date Your Wife* will positively alter thousands of couple's futures. As a husband for 38 years, I applaud Justin Buzzard's work and I would put it in the hands of every man I could!"

> **Wayne Cordeiro,** Senior Pastor, New Hope Christian Fellowship, Honolulu, Hawaii

"I need a book like this! I'm often in fits and starts trying to regularly date my wife, so I'm glad the Lord has given Justin Buzzard the vision and insight to write *Date Your Wife* for strugglers like me!"

> **Thabiti Anyabwile,** Senior Pastor, First Baptist Church of Grand Cayman; author, *The Decline of African American Theology*

"Men, we desperately need this book, and our wives desperately need us to read it. This isn't just a book about marriage, it's a book about being a man who loves the gospel, lives the gospel, and leads his wife and children with the gospel. Married or single, young or old—if you're a man—get this book, read this book, and then get a copy for every man you know."

> **Burk Parsons,** Associate Pastor, Saint Andrew's Chapel, Sanford, Florida; editor, *Tabletalk* magazine

"I am *thrilled* about this book for several reasons. First of all, my brother, Justin, thoroughly gets the gospel of God's grace, and it decorates every page of this book. Second, he's intentional about loving his wife well, and, therefore, we need Justin's tribe to increase *exponentially*. Third, his book is so incredibly practical. He's left me without excuse! Last, Justin's writing, heart, and wisdom make me so glad to know that Jesus is the spouse I always wanted, and that, by his grace, I can love my wife as he loves me. This book, like my brother, rocks!"

> **Scotty Smith,** Founding Pastor, Christ Community Church, Franklin, Tennessee; author, *Everyday Prayers* and *The Reign of Grace*

"For a young, married man like myself, this is a much needed reminder! *Date Your Wife* encourages me to man up, trust Jesus, and love my wife well. I encourage all husbands to go grab a copy."

Trip Lee, rapper; author

"I am a big fan of Justin Buzzard and this book. I champion any call for men to step out of passivity and dominate the things that matter most—*Date Your Wife* beckons me as a man to do just that. The primacy of being a great husband is undeniable in Scripture and I appreciate this gospel-centered, practical, and powerful resource to help us men step up in the most noble of all roles. I pray God uses *Date Your Wife* to call up a generation of men who are first and foremost great husbands. I can think of no greater gift to our children, our churches, and our cities than men whose wives are pursued well and have marriages that flourish and go the distance."

John Wiley Bryson, Co-Founder and Teaching Pastor, Fellowship Memphis, Memphis, Tennessee; Leadership Coach, Fellowship Associates

"Otis Redding sang 'Try a little tenderness' and some husbands want to—but don't know how. Justin Buzzard gives sound theological and practical advice. If more husbands learn to date their wives and, through God's grace, truly love them, many marriages will be saved."

Marvin Olasky, Editor-in-chief, *World Magazine*

"Justin reveals a gift for combining challenge with encouragement. In *Date Your Wife*, he manages to propose provocative and practical ideas without making me feel like a marriage dunce. So, I hereby confer to Justin the title of 'Professor of Creative Marriage.' May his students learn well!"

Greg Spencer, Professor of Communication Studies, Westmont College; author, *Awakening the Quieter Virtues*

DATE YOUR WIFE

A HUSBAND'S GUIDE

DATE YOUR WIFE

JUSTIN BUZZARD

:: CROSSWAY®

WHEATON, ILLINOIS

Date Your Wife

Copyright © 2012 by Justin Buzzard

Published by Crossway
        1300 Crescent Street
        Wheaton, Illinois 60187

Cover design: Josh Dennis

Cover image(s): John Wilson, illustrator

First printing 2012

Printed in the United States of America

Scripture quotations are from the ESV® Bible (The Holy Bible, English Standard Version®), copyright © 2001 by Crossway, a publishing ministry of Good News Publishers. Used by permission. All rights reserved.

All emphases in Scripture quotations have been added by the author.

Trade paperback ISBN: 978-1-4335-3135-4
PDF ISBN: 978-1-4335-3136-1
Mobipocket ISBN: 978-1-4335-3137-8
ePub ISBN: 978-1-4335-3138-5

Library of Congress Cataloging-in-Publication Data

Buzzard, Justin, 1978-
  Date your wife / Justin Buzzard.
    p. cm.
  Includes bibliographical references (p. 143) and indexes.
  ISBN 978-1-4335-3135-4 (tp)
  1. Husbands—Religious life. 2. Marriage—Religious aspects—Christianity. 3. Wives—Psychology. I. Title.
BV4528.3.B89   2012
248.8425—dc23   2012001370

Crossway is a publishing ministry of Good News Publishers.

VP		29	28	27	26	25	24	23	22	21	
23	22	21	20	19	18	17	16	15	14	13	12

Enjoy life with the wife
whom you love, all the . . . days of your life.
Ecclesiastes 9:9

CONTENTS

PART 4: THE PERFECT

ACKNOWLEDGMENTS

I want to thank my mom for planting in me a big vision for manhood and marriage well before I hit puberty or could tie my shoes. Mom, your fingerprints are all over this book.

I want to thank my dad for his example of learning how to date his wife all over again after twenty years of marriage. Dad, you've taught me more than you know about the power of grace and what it means to be a man.

I want to thank the people of Garden City Church for being excited about my writing this book while simultaneously starting our life together as a new church plant.

Above all I want to thank my bride and best friend, Taylor, for filling my life and our testosterone-crazed home with so much joy. Life has felt new, wonderfully different and new, since the day we met. Taylor, you are God's greatest gift to me, and the road ahead looks so exciting. I love you. I feel the way the nineteenth-century British preacher Charles Spurgeon felt:

> Matrimony came from Paradise, and leads to it. I never was half so happy, before I was a married man, as I am now. When you are married, your bliss begins. Let the husband love his wife as he loves himself, and a little better, for she is his better half. He should feel, "If there's only one good wife in the whole world, I've got her."[1]

13

Finally, years ago Jesus changed my life. Ultimately, this is a book about Jesus, the man who gives us men the grace and the power to be real men in a world full of fake men. Jesus, thank you for saving me and giving me a new life. Jesus, use this book to make men new and to breathe fresh life into marriages.

PREFACE

Why You ~~Should Read~~ Want to Read This Book

I want you to do something. Make a list in your head of the marriages you've seen that you actually like. How many married couples can you think of that have a thriving marriage—a good, happy, alive marriage—the kind of marriage that makes other people want to get married?

How many marriages did you think of?

I've tried this question on many people. Most people can come up with only one or two examples of strong, lively, and attractive marriages. This book aims to change that. Things don't have to stay the way they are.[1]

You know the statistics. Marriage is broken in our world. If your marriage isn't broken, the marriage of someone you know is. At the very least, your marriage isn't pulsating with the life and power it was meant to have.

But it's not too late. There's still hope for marriage—for your marriage, for your neighbor's marriage, and for marriages that haven't happened yet. Marriages can be jump-started; the sacred union between a husband and a wife can receive new life and power. I don't care who you are, who you've been, or what your marriage has been through—everything can be made new. It's harder and easier than you think.

Men, it starts with you. You and I and the men we know want something more. Perhaps you've settled for a marriage that looks like most other marriages. Perhaps you now look like most other husbands—ordinary, nice, confused. But what you really want is a marriage that feels like a mission, a marriage that's moving forward toward something exciting, mysterious, and grand—kind of like the way dating felt.

Men, this book is for you. Pick it up and read it.

PART ONE

THE GOOD

1

HOW YOUR MARRIAGE STARTED

From as far back as I can remember I've thought about marriage. My daydreams and prayers have always been full of thoughts about "her."

Beginning at the age of four or five, my mom tucked me in at night with prayers that made mention of my future wife. We prayed for her protection and well-being. We didn't know who this little girl was or where she lived, but we asked God to arrange all the details for us to someday meet, marry, and build a family of our own.

Twenty years after these prayers started, I met "her," the woman of my dreams, at a party in Palo Alto, California. Seven months later I proposed. Three months after that we were married. Last week my bride of seven years gave birth to our third son, giving us three boys under age four. We've been busy.

My story is rare. Most men don't grow up with a mom who tucked them in at night breathing out sentences and prayers about the grand adventure of being a husband. But the rest of my story is not rare. Every man's marriage begins just like mine—with a date and a dream.

THE GOOD

A DATE

Your marriage didn't start on your wedding day. Husband, your marriage started on your first date. During that first date with your bride, you began laying the foundation for the day you would say, "I do." You began laying the foundation your marriage stands upon today.

How long have you been married? How long ago was that first date? Think back to that day. Replay the memories in your mind. Most men don't realize that the concept of dating their wife is something they've already built into the foundation of their marriage.

My wife's name is Taylor. We met in a kitchen (I'll tell you that story later). Our first date happened six weeks later in a redwood forest.

I called Taylor on a Friday at 9:00 a.m. It was raining outside. I cleared my throat just before she answered the phone. I told her I wanted to take her out on a date. She asked, "When?" I said, "Now." I told Taylor I wanted to take her for a hike in the rain. She paused, stuttered, then asked if she could call me back in ten minutes.

Ten minutes later, Taylor called back and said yes. She lived in San Francisco and I lived in San Jose, so I had us meet halfway, in Palo Alto, the same city where we'd first met six weeks earlier. The image is burned into my mind of blonde Taylor in her blue jeans and pink button-down standing under the neon lights of the Stanford Theater on University Avenue waiting for me to arrive. I had never been so excited to be with a girl.

Taylor stepped into my Jeep and our first date began. I

drove us up a winding road to a redwood forest in the Santa Cruz Mountains. We spent the next two hours strolling along a trail in the forest getting to know each other while a soft drizzle fell on our rain jackets. Eventually we found ourselves next to a fallen tree trunk covered in moss. We sat on the mossy log and kept talking. I didn't know it then, but six months later I would get down on one knee and propose to Taylor at this mossy log.

After the hike we stopped for soup and coffee. We discovered that five years earlier we had both vacationed with our families at the same hotel in Idaho during the last week of December, but our paths never crossed. I couldn't tell what Taylor was thinking about me. When I dropped Taylor off at her car, I handed her a book I had purposely brought along, *Desiring God* by John Piper. I pretended that the book just happened to be sitting on my backseat. I casually glanced back at the book, then handed it to Taylor, telling her I thought she'd like it because of how it related to many of the things we talked about during our walk in the woods. I told her that the book meant a lot to me. The real reason I gave her the book was so that, even if she didn't like me, she'd at least be obligated to see me one more time to give me back my book. It wasn't until after we were married that I learned Taylor drove home that day and told her roommate she believed I was the man she would marry.

That was our first date. I remember it like it happened yesterday.

What was your first date with your wife like? Think about it. Where were you? What did you do? What did you talk about?

What did you learn? What were you feeling? What was she wearing? How did your date happen in the first place?

No first date is exactly alike. Each of us has a different first date story. But we all have a story.

My dad's story is that he took my mom out for pizza in downtown Sacramento, then he took her out dancing. It was a blind date. They had never met before. The date worked.

My friend Campbell's story is that after months of friendship and hanging out, he finally got over his nerves, took his "friend" to a park on a moonlit night, gave her a rose, and told her he felt something more than friendship and wanted to start pursuing her.

What's your story?

My assumption is that all of our first date stories have one thing in common: we acted like men. We pursued our wives-to-be. We made the move. We initiated. We took a risk. We took the lead.

Husbands, this is important for us to remember. Throughout this book I'm calling you to do one thing. The action I want you to take is summed up in just three words: date your wife. This three-word action isn't something foreign, intimidating, or new—I'm asking us to do something we've already done, something we've already built into the foundation of our marriages—to date our wives.

Even if you haven't been on a bike in years, you still know how to ride one. It's the same with dating your wife. My aim is to get men back on the bike and to get us there in the best shape of our lives, exercising the best possible form.

A DREAM

Can you remember when you first began thinking about marriage? Most women can. Most men can't.

I've met women who had the flavor of their wedding cakes picked out when they were in preschool. My wife's not one of them. A child of divorce, she thought little of marriage—she was scared of marriage. She planned to pursue a career and put marriage off until her late thirties. That plan didn't work. Taylor was twenty-three on our wedding day.

I've met men who think a lot about women but seem to never think about "the woman," about marriage. That's not my story. I grew up looking at girls with one question in the front of my mind, "Could I marry her?" One girl passed the test.

Whether your story is more like my wife's or more like mine, the point is that you didn't approach your first date or your wedding day with a blank slate. You had thought about marriage before. Whether highly conscious or unconscious of it, you had ideas, feelings, and beliefs about marriage. You had a dream.

A dream is a collection of ideas, feelings, and beliefs about a particular topic. A dream is what drives a man. As a boy grows up, he gradually forms a dream for his future marriage. Some men are aware of this, some men are not. Some men form a healthy dream for marriage, some men do not. But every man approaches his first date and his wedding day driven by a dream.

What was your dream?

Some men dream about marrying a woman who will satisfy their every desire, preference, and need.

Some men form an antidream; they simply dream of a

marriage that is not like their parents' marriage (or lack of marriage). Early on, they decide they want a wife who is not like Mom. They decide they want to be a man who is not like Dad.

Some men dream of a marriage that is conflict-free or not a lot of work.

Some men dream of a marriage that honors God and that is a lot of fun.

The dream that drove you to that first date, that drove you to the altar, is likely still driving your marriage today. That dream set the course, and is probably still setting the course, of your marriage. What was, what is, that dream?

If we are going to be men who date our wives, we must uncover the dream that drives us. The way to uncover something is to ask more questions.

Take a few minutes to think through these questions:

What is the earliest memory of marriage that you can think of? How has that memory influenced you?

Who taught you about marriage? Who taught you about what it means to be a man and how that's different from what it means to be a woman? What did these teachers teach you?

What is the healthiest, happiest marriage you've ever seen? What made that marriage so attractive?

What is the most dysfunctional marriage you've ever seen? What made that marriage so unattractive?

What kind of a man was your dad? What kind of a relationship did you/do you have with him? If we were having coffee together, what would you tell me about what it was like growing up as his son?

What is your greatest fear for your marriage?

What is your greatest frustration with yourself, with your wife, and with your marriage?

What is your wife's greatest complaint about being married to you? What does she appreciate most about being married to you?

What is your greatest hope for your marriage? What do you really want to see happen in you, in your marriage, and in your life before you die? How's it going to happen?

You just deconstructed the dream that's been driving your marriage. Each answer to the questions above represents one piece of the dream that drives how you operate as a husband. All the pieces don't make complete sense yet. Right now we're staring at an engine that's been taken apart. The aim of this book is to make better sense of these different pieces, to do some cleanup work, and then to rebuild the engine to run better than before.

We are in this together. Don't read this book with only your marriage in mind. Let's keep in mind our neighbor down the street and our friend at work. Men, together we are jump-starting the modern marriage.

TAKE ACTION

1. Commit to praying that God would jump-start your marriage and the marriage of one other man you have regular contact with. Even if you're not a praying man, I suggest you get on your knees and pray right now.

2. Re-create your first date with your wife. It doesn't need to be exactly like your first date; just do whatever you can to relive that first date. Schedule this to happen within the next three weeks. Before the sun goes down tonight, put this date on your calendar and your wife's calendar.

3. Spend some more time looking at your answers to the questions above. Are there any important connections or themes you notice in your answers?

2

WHO INVENTED MARRIAGE, AND WHY?

My oldest son is named Crusoe, but from day one we've called him "Cru." We named him after Robinson Crusoe, the hero of Daniel Defoe's novel about a bad man who becomes a good man while shipwrecked on a remote island with his Bible, some guns, and a few supplies.[1] In the story, God turns Crusoe into a new man as Crusoe reads his Bible with new eyes, finally discovering the love God gives to men who don't deserve it. Taylor and I spend a lot of time talking to Cru about where his name comes from and about the God who can remake him. Cru is starting to get it.

What Cru is not getting is marriage. Cru is four years old, and he remains dead set on marrying his mommy. I keep telling him how that would be disgusting, that his mom is already taken, and that when he is twenty-four his mom will be fifty and he will be more interested in premenopausal women. Cru doesn't care. He wants to marry Mommy.

Cru will grow out of this. In the meantime, I'm teaching him about how marriage was invented. This is where education about anything should start, at the beginning.

THE INVENTION

Have you ever thought about this? How would you tell a four-year-old the story of how marriage was invented? We know the stories about the lightbulb, the combustion engine, and the telephone—these inventions came from human hands after years of trial and error. Do we know the story about marriage?

In 1764 a man named Joe went for a walk in his field. After a long day working his farm, Joe needed to think. With the sun setting and his muscles aching, Joe walked west and again turned his thoughts towards his "idea." He'd been thinking about it for almost a year, though he hadn't told anybody. People wondered what Joe was working on; he now spent so much time doodling strange drawings, pacing his home, and taking these long walks in his field. Joe still wasn't sure if his idea would work, and he was afraid of what people would think. He didn't even have a name for his idea yet.

It had been long enough. Tomorrow, Joe decided, he would test out his idea. Joe marched home a determined man, his heart beating with fear and excitement. He barely slept that night. The next morning Joe quickly dressed himself in his best clothes and made his way to the village square where he knew he'd see "her."

There she was, standing near the butcher's shop—Jenny, the woman Joe couldn't stop thinking about. It was now or never. Joe approached Jenny. Jenny turned toward Joe. Joe got down on one knee, took Jenny by the hand, and asked if she would let him love her (and her alone) and if, in turn, she would love him back, sharing her love with no other man. Jenny looked confused and intrigued. Joe told Jenny that if she said yes to this, he thought it would work best if they lived together in the same house. He told her that this new relationship would be a big commitment, one that would last until death. Joe told Jenny he had invented some names for all this—that he'd like to call her "wife," that she could call him "husband," and that they could call their relationship "marriage." Joe said he was sure this would catch on, that once they tried it many other men and women from their village and beyond would want to try this out. Sweat poured down Joe's face, his eyes eager for Jenny's answer.

Jenny cried. This was the most beautiful idea she'd ever heard. She quickly said yes. Joe shouted a sound of happiness that was heard throughout the town square.

Within weeks, Joe and Jenny created a ceremony that marked the start of their marriage. They invited the whole village to attend. Jenny wore a white dress. They spoke their commitments to each other, "vows" they called them. They gave each other rings as gifts. They kissed, they danced, they went on a "honeymoon," and everyone celebrated. Before the end of the year, ten other men and ten other women decided to try out Joe's invention. Soon it was heard that in neighboring villages, and even far away in the city, other people were "getting married." Joe couldn't believe how well his invention had worked.

Marriage had a beginning. There was a time when marriage was not. But Joe didn't invent marriage. If marriage had been invented in 1764 by a guy named Joe, then marriage would deserve the esteem we give to other two-hundred-and-fifty-year-old inventions like the spinning wheel and bifocals—wonderful inventions, but not something you want to read a book about. A marriage is one of the few things we see every day that was not invented by humans.

THE GOOD

Your marriage has a richer history than your first date, your boyhood dreams, and Joe's daring move back in 1764. The roots of your marriage run deep. Real deep.

THE LOOK

Do you remember the first time you looked at your wife? For some of us men, that first look changed the course of our lives. Did you know that the very first time a man looked at a woman, marriage happened?

I looked at Taylor and my life changed. I love this story. I don't have any other like it.

On an ordinary Friday night I drove to Palo Alto to hang out with Dave. First I stopped by James's house. James was throwing a party at his two-story bachelor pad, just down the street from Stanford. I planned to stay for a few minutes to say hi to James and a few other friends, then I'd spend the evening with my buddy Dave. I walked through the front door, made my way through the crowd, and entered the kitchen. Then it happened.

I stepped onto the linoleum floor. Ten feet in front of me stood this stunning blue-eyed, blonde-haired woman with the happiest smile I'd ever seen. I don't know if this makes sense, but she was so fun looking. She was so joyful, so energetic, so beautiful—like nothing I'd ever seen before. This was the first time the phrase "drop-dead gorgeous" made sense to me. There was something about this woman; I looked at her once and I couldn't stop. It was like a spell came over me. I didn't notice anything else in the room. Without thinking, I walked up and introduced myself to her. With a slight stutter, one she'd had since childhood and that still shows up now and then when she's nervous, she told me her name was "T—Ta—Taylor." Within minutes the spell deepened as I discovered Taylor's personality and her obvious love for Jesus. Immediately I called Dave. I told him I'd met a girl and that he and I wouldn't be hanging out that night. That first look at Taylor changed the trajectory of my life. It's the reason why I'm writing this book.

God invented this. God created a man. Then God created a woman. Then God "brought her to the man" (Gen. 2:22) and, with one look at the woman, the man fell in love.

THE FIRST WEDDING

As the father of the bride, God walks Eve down the aisle in the garden of Eden and presents her to Adam. Adam looks at Eve. Next, Adam speaks the first human words recorded in the Bible. At first sight of the bride God brings, Adam speaks his first words. Adam's first speech is poetry—a declaration of excitement and homecoming over the sight of "woman" with whom he is "at last" (finally!) united (Gen. 2:23). Two sentences later we learn that the groom and the bride are standing before each other naked and unashamed—they don't have any clothes on and they don't have any shame on. The first man and the first woman stand before each other and before God as a naked, shame-free, happily married couple. All it took was one look.

The first time a man looked at a woman, marriage happened. Adam and Eve didn't invent this. Joe didn't invent this. God invented this. It was God's brilliant idea to create man, to create woman, and join them in marriage—this unique union that begins with a look and quickly escalates into shouts of joy, nakedness, uninhibited freedom, and a closeness so magical it's described as becoming "one flesh."

Most every man I know wants something like this: a beautiful woman over whom he shouts for joy, gets naked, and experiences shameless freedom and mysterious closeness. The problem is that most men don't see that the place to find this is within marriage. Most men don't know that these deep longings come from God, from what God invented thousands of years ago in the garden of Eden when he turned dust into a man, a rib into a woman, and a man and a woman into a husband and a wife.[2]

This is why I'm teaching Cru the story of how marriage was invented. Before this decade is over, Cru will start to feel the longing. He will wake up to powerful desires pulsating through his mind, his heart, and his body. He will look at women in a new way. He won't want to marry Mommy anymore.[3]

Long before Cru wakes up to the longing, I want Cru awake to the story. Only the story can set a man free to make sense out of what churns inside him. I want my oldest son to know that once upon a time God created marriage, the relationship of relationships, where a man can finally give life to the poetry hidden in his heart. Every man is a poet, wanting to give expression to the deep things in his heart. Most of us men simply don't know, or have long forgotten, that God invented marriage to do just this. Five hundred years ago Martin Luther said it, "There is no bond on earth so sweet, nor any separation so bitter, as that which occurs in a good marriage."[4] Most of us men have forgotten that we come to life only as we bond our life, give away our life, to a woman. Most of us men have forgotten that to live this life that we were created to live, a miracle must happen.

TAKE ACTION

1. Read Genesis chapter 2. What do you see in this first marriage that you want more of in your marriage? Read this chapter with your wife and ask her the same question.

2. Approach your wife with fresh eyes this week. Whenever you encounter her (whether in a moment of joy or a moment of conflict), look at her as though you're looking at her for the first time. Look at your bride. What do you see?

3. Share this book with another man (perhaps with the man/ marriage you've been praying for). Tell this man what you've been discovering.

PART TWO

THE BAD

3

WHERE MARRIAGES GO WRONG, PART I: THE HUSBAND

Once word got out that I'm writing a book called *Date Your Wife*, people began sending me advice to include in the book. So far it is all sex advice. And so far, these e-mails have all come from women. I don't know why all the e-mails are about sex and why they're all from women. (FYI, women don't normally e-mail me about sex, though I encourage my wife to do so as often as she likes.) Here is an e-mail I received last Friday:

Hi Justin,

I thought you might be interested to know I went to a Moms' homeschooling meeting last week and the topic was intimacy with your husband. Three different ladies presented on the importance of having regular sex with your husband: 3-day rule (never go 3 days without having sex) and 2x a week rule (have sex at least 2x a week). They all had experience and research to support how it benefits the entire family, and changed one family from almost divorced to happy as can be. I hope this is not too weird I am emailing you about this. Thought it may be useful for your book.[1]

This e-mail shocked me.

You might be shocked by what shocked me. It all depends on how you handle sex in your marriage.

I was shocked to read that a group of wives are getting excited about the idea that sex with their husbands has many benefits and should be done twice a week. If we need to go to a moms' homeschooling meeting to learn that sex is really important in a marriage and in a family, we're in big trouble. I don't need to see any research about the benefits of sex for a marriage; I just know it feels really good and that when a husband and wife really love and like each other, they get naked and have a lot of sex. Back when you were dating your wife, as you were heading toward marriage, did you need anyone to tell you that you should have lots of sex together?

In our marriage we don't have a three-day rule, we have something called a three-day exception. Only if I'm traveling will we make an exception and go three days without doing what Adam and Eve did on their wedding day.[2] No one needed to tell Adam and Eve to have more sex. But, in our fallen world, some of us need reminding. Of all the issues that the apostle Paul could have addressed with the dysfunctional Corinthian church, he highlighted the importance of regular (I think, frequent) sexual intimacy as a central part of marriage, selflessness, and spiritual warfare.[3]

Taylor was as surprised as I was by the e-mail. She responded to the woman with an e-mail of her own:

Personally, I think the 2x a week rule and 3-day rule isn't frequent enough. I think aiming for every other day (4x a week) is a healthier range. But, I guess this is a question our husbands can best answer, since they typically have the bigger "sex tank," and we definitely don't want to send them out into this sex-crazed world with their sex tanks on low. Satan is prowling. One other brief thought is that when I'm aiming for 4x a week, that doesn't have to be roses, chocolate, and lingerie encounters every time. Quickies are an ace in our pockets. :)

Taylor[4]

Man, I love my wife.

Quick Survey:
1. Currently, how many times a week do you have sex with your wife?
2. Ideally, how many times a week would you like to have sex with your wife?
3. What needs to change in your marriage to bridge the gap between question 1 and question 2?
4. How would your wife answer these questions for herself?

What the two e-mails above have in common is that they're both wife-driven attempts at sustaining and improving a marriage. Every marriage involves two people, so (except in the rarest of cases) both husband and wife are responsible for the problems in their marriage. And both husband and wife are responsible for addressing those problems and moving the marriage forward. But, this isn't a book for women. This is a book for men. And this book is fueled by this conviction: if you want to change a marriage, change the man.

THE BAD

THE PROBLEM

Underline this next sentence. If you want to change a marriage, change the man. That's you. So, whether you've been following the two-times-a-week rule, the one-time-a-week rule, or the one-time-a-quarter rule in your marriage, don't rush to show your wife my wife's e-mail. That won't work. Your wife isn't the problem. You're the problem. I'm the problem. Men are the problem. If you want to change a marriage, change the man. If you want to change your marriage, you must first see that you are the main problem in your marriage.

I imagine there are exceptions to this, but you and your marriage are not the exception. There's probably one guy somewhere in Canada who can legitimately claim that most of the problems in his marriage stem from his Canadian wife. He's the exception. You aren't. The man who reads this book and disagrees, who thinks his wife is the main problem in the marriage, is the man who most needs to read this book.

What's wrong with your marriage? What's broken? Think back to some of your answers at the end of chapter 1. If you had to summarize it in a single sentence, what's wrong with your marriage? Write that sentence down.

Men across the globe just wrote thousands of different answers to that question. Men, that's not good. We don't need a sentence to answer the question. All we need is one word. And, men, we should all have the same answer. Let's try this again.

What's wrong with your marriage?

Me.

Me!

I am what is wrong with my marriage.

You are what is wrong with your marriage.

It's your fault. This is the second most important truth to learn from this book: it's your fault. You are the husband. You are the man. And God has given man the ability to be the best thing or the worst thing that ever happened to a marriage. Before you can be the best thing that ever happened to your marriage, you must see that you have always been the worst thing that happened to your marriage. If you want to change a marriage, change the man. Why? Because the man is what is wrong, and the man is what, made right, alters the course of everything.

THE JOB

Before God gave the first man a wife, he gave him a job. God took the man, put him in a garden, and there gave the man a twofold mission:

> The LORD God took the man and put him in the garden of Eden to *work it* and *keep it*. (Gen. 2:15)

Fundamental to his manhood, God gave Adam this double calling: work and keep. These Hebrew verbs can be better translated: cultivate and guard. God commissioned the first man to cultivate the garden and guard the garden. God gave the first man immense responsibility, immense power, to cause the garden to flourish or to fade.

God gave this to you, too. God gave you this same calling, this same responsibility, this same power. Your ancestry goes all the way back to Adam. We are all related to the first man. We are men and, whatever garden God has put us in, we have been put there to cultivate and guard that garden. To be a man is to be entrusted with enormous privilege and responsibility. To be a man is to be a cultivator and guardian. To be a man is to know God put you on this planet to cause life to flourish.

God created Adam and God created you to cultivate and guard.

And Adam screwed it all up.

And so have we.

God gave Adam a job before he gave him a wife. So, when God presented Adam with his bride, what did Adam know he was called to do as a husband? If you had to summarize it in a sentence, what was Adam called to do for his marriage and for his wife?

Cultivate it and guard it.

This is exactly what the first husband failed to do. Adam failed to cultivate his wife—he didn't cause her to flourish. Adam failed to guard his wife—he didn't protect her from danger.

To date your wife is to cultivate and guard her. Dating your wife means to cultivate and guard your wife and your marriage.[5] Cultivate it and guard it. You haven't done it. One way or another, you and I are just like Adam. We've failed to be the man that God has created and commissioned us to be.

What's wrong with your marriage? Until you can authentically answer, "Me," until you can feel that answer deep in your guts, this book won't help you or your marriage.

TAKE ACTION

1. Ask God to show you, very specifically, how you have been the biggest problem in your marriage.

2. Take your wife on a date and speak two powerful words to her: "I'm sorry." Before this week is over, make time to confess your list to your wife, the list of ways you've hurt her and failed to cultivate and guard her. Ask for your wife's forgiveness and God's forgiveness. Cultivate a new habit of being the first person to say "I'm sorry" in your marriage. This can only be done through God's grace and power, so rely on God's strength, not your own.

3. Make love to your wife.

4. Repeat steps 1–3 for the rest of your marriage.

4

WHERE MARRIAGES GO WRONG, PART II: THE HUSBAND'S RELIGION

Earlier this year an old friend called me late one night. I took the call on the back patio so that I wouldn't wake up my family. The stars were bright, but my friend's voice was sad. If sadness, shame, and anger make a sound when mixed together, that's the sound I heard on the other end of the phone. Before I heard the news, I knew it would be bad.

My friend took a deep breath. Then he told me. He had just found out his wife was having an affair with another man.

Ten years of marriage. Three kids. Then an affair.

The affair had been going on for months. The news knocked the life out of my friend and knocked the wind out of me. He and his wife were now living separately. The kids were asking questions.

He wanted the marriage to work. He wasn't sure if she did. We decided to spend an upcoming weekend together to talk and pray through it all. That weekend I watched a miracle start to happen.

Have you ever looked into the eyes of a grown man who just found out he was physically and emotionally betrayed by the person he loved the most? Have you ever looked into the eyes of a grown man and watched the sting of betrayal transition into sharp conviction over his own failures? My friend was furious over the affair. But he was more furious with himself. The pain of the affair awakened him to realities he had been hiding from—uncomfortable realities about who he was as a man and as a husband. A miracle began surfacing.

My old friend proceeded to tell me the ten-year story of his marriage. It was a story I didn't know, and it was a story he didn't know. He had never seen his story this way before, and he had never told this story to anybody. It was the story of Adam.

ADAM'S STORY

God gave Adam work to do, a purpose and calling for his life. "Cultivate and guard this garden I've given you; cause life to flourish. Take the raw materials of this garden and develop them—build, invent, create—so that new life will flourish and thrive in this environment. Develop and protect what I'm entrusting to you," God said to Adam.

Then the climax. After giving Adam a calling, God gave Adam a wife—the crown jewel of his calling. "Cultivate and protect this woman I've given you; cause life to flourish. Take the raw materials of this marriage and develop them—build, invent, create—so that your wife will flourish and thrive in this environment. Cultivate and guard what I'm entrusting to you," God said to Adam.

Central to Adam's calling as a husband was the call to

cultivate and guard his wife so that she would flourish, so that their sacred union would thrive. God called Adam to date his wife. God didn't present Adam to Eve. He presented Eve to Adam. God put the woman in the man's hands, having already told the man to handle with care the gift he would be given.

Quick Assessment:
1. Is your wife flourishing under your care?
2. How would friends and family answer this question?
3. How would your wife answer this question?

How would the first husband have scored on this assessment?

Immediately after the romance of the first wedding day, a false lover shows up. The story immediately moves from "the man and his wife were both naked and were not ashamed" to a false lover conversing with Adam's wife. One sentence after the celebration and the sex, a Serpent slips into the garden. The garden—the garden that was Adam's to guard—now has an intruder.

The intruder heads straight for Adam's most cherished charge. This seductive intruder is crafty. He has a way with words. Posing and speaking as though he has the woman's best interest at heart, the Serpent—Satan himself—entices Adam's wife to doubt God and disobey him. He tempts and tells Eve to make a choice that he says will fulfill her but will really empty her. Eve takes the bait. Eve bites. And Eve tastes sadness, guilt, and insecurity for the first time in human history. The wife who stood naked and unashamed now stands naked and ashamed.

Where was Adam? The Bible puts it simply and starkly: "Her husband . . . was with her" (Gen. 3:6).

Adam was with Eve. But he didn't do anything. Adam was

supposed to guard the garden and guard his wife. The second he spotted the Serpent, Adam should've crushed the Serpent. He should've rushed straight toward the intruder and eliminated him, keeping his wife safe and sound. But Adam just stood there. He let the Serpent in. He let the lethal lover talk to his wife. He listened to their seductive and sinful conversation. He watched as his wife made the worst choice of her life. He just stood there. The cultivator. The guardian. He just stood there.

When Adam first looked at Eve he fell in love. This time Adam looked at Eve and withheld his love. He stood still, abandoning his wife, his calling, and his manhood.

The first husband had a job to do that he didn't do.

OUR STORY

This failure to cultivate and guard his wife is what gutted my friend. He learned that his Eve had been with another man, and this ripped him up inside. Her sin hurt him like he'd never been hurt before. But in taking a fresh look at their ten years together, he realized that he'd spent the past decade standing in Adam's footprints. He spotted ten years of overgrowth, ten years of failing to tend and guard the garden.

My friend had thought he had a decent marriage. He was committed to his wife. He went to church. Though he worked long hours, he spent time with his family on the weekends. He meant what he said when he said his wedding vows. But the story of the decent man with the decent marriage didn't add up anymore. My friend began seeing his story as a repeat of Adam's story. He began seeing himself in Adam.

Committed is the word my friend kept using. He told me

how he'd always been committed as a husband, how he'd always done his duty. Our weekend began with these speeches of how he had done his job as a husband because he had been a committed husband. His equation looked like this:

Committed husband = A husband who has done his job

Commitment is good. We want to be committed husbands. The problem was how my friend defined commitment and how this definition ruled his sense of what it means to be a husband. He defined "committed husband" as a man who isn't going anywhere. Again, this is good. We want to be husbands who don't go anywhere else, husbands who remain monogamous and faithful. But this is an incomplete picture of what it means to be a husband. Committed husband: a man who isn't going anywhere. So, my friend's equation looked like this:

A man who isn't going anywhere = A husband who has done his job

Using this measurement, Adam was a good husband. Adam didn't go anywhere. He just stood there. Adam was committed to Eve. He didn't have an interest in another woman. Adam did his job.

See, the problem with the modern marriage goes deeper than the husband. The source of the problem isn't the husband, the source of the problem is the husband's belief system. My friend's marriage was broken because what he believed was broken.

THE BAD

RELIGION

What you believe will drive how you live. Every husband has a belief system that drives his life and marriage. For ten years my friend woke up every morning with this belief: if I remain staunchly committed to not going anywhere else as a husband, my wife will be okay, my marriage will be okay, and I will be okay—I will have done my job. This belief powered the first decade of their marriage. The problem with this belief is that God invented marriage. And these are not the instructions the divine Inventor gave for how to handle his invention. God gave us men a far bigger, far more exciting, and far more costly vision for marriage and for our calling as husbands.

Religion is easy. Religion is manageable. Religion is working hard at something in order to earn acceptance, approval, and the life you think you deserve because of your obedient performance. Many people think Christianity is a religion. People think the Bible teaches that if you work hard at being staunchly committed to God, he will accept you and reward you. This is what my friend thought. Religion governed how he approached God and how he approached his wife. He thought if he lived as a basically good person, then he would earn God's favor and get the decent life he deserved. He thought if he stayed committed to his wife and didn't go anywhere, then God would give him a decent marriage with decent sex in a decent American town with a decent church down the street. The problem is that everything he believed about God didn't come from God. It wasn't true. And everything he believed about marriage didn't come from the Inventor of marriage. It wasn't true.

Somewhere along the way he started believing in religion

instead of believing in God. Somewhere along the way he started believing in being a good roommate instead of being a good husband. Somewhere along the way he started believing that being a good husband was up to him—that he could do it in his own strength and power. Then his wife had sex with another man. That broke the spell.

During our weekend together I watched a man wake up from a deep sleep. His eyes started to open. He could see. His decent marriage wasn't working out the way it was supposed to work out. His religion wasn't giving him the life he thought he deserved. His god wasn't doing what he told him to do. He slowly started spotting the counterfeit. Pain does that. It gives you new eyes, eyes to see the counterfeit foundations you've been standing on.

The foundation, the beliefs my friend had built his life on, shattered beneath him. Religion didn't work. Committed husband didn't work. For the first time in his life my friend realized that he couldn't do it. He was desperate. It felt like drowning. He didn't think he could save his marriage or save himself. He didn't think he had what it took to fix this.

I told him he was right.

I told him God had him right where he wanted him.

Drowning. Desperation. Knowing you can't save yourself. Knowing you can't save your marriage. Knowing you don't have the power to be the husband God calls you to be. Knowing that to cultivate and guard the garden will require from you something you don't have the ability to give—to love a woman you've not loved well for ten years, a woman who has just hurt you so sharply. That's when a husband wakes up to what a beautifully fearsome thing God invented when he invented marriage. A man comes alive when he finally feels in his guts that religion can't fuel his life or his marriage, when he makes the painfully sweet discovery that there is only one fuel source that can get the engine running again: grace.

It's a miracle.

My friend and I talked late into the night. We wondered if this is what Adam felt. We wondered if this is what the first husband felt after the great failure in the garden. When, immediately after the failure, God showed up in the garden. When, naked and afraid, Adam hid behind a tree. And the sound of God's footsteps came closer and closer. And suddenly, God's pursuing voice called out, "Where are you, Adam?" (See Gen. 3:8–9).[1]

TAKE ACTION

1. Decipher the deep beliefs that drive you as a man and as a husband. Think about other husbands you know. What beliefs seem to drive their marriages? How is religion different from grace?
2. Take your wife out to dinner and ask her the questions from the end of chapter 1. Let her know that you're asking these questions because you want to know her better. Listen well.
3. Memorize Proverbs 18:22, "He who finds a wife finds a good thing and obtains favor from the LORD."

5

WHERE MARRIAGES GO WRONG, PART III: THE HUSBAND'S ACTION

Men are idiots. Men work hard to date and pursue their girlfriend, but once they marry their girlfriend, it all stops. The man who dated, wooed, and passionately pursued his girlfriend degenerates into the husband who merely shares a home, bills, conflict, and problems with his wife.

Think about it. Once upon a time there was a girl you really liked. And you put a lot of effort into impressing that girl. Eventually, that girl became your girlfriend. You told your friends all about her. You were happy. You kept at it. You didn't let anything get in the way of impressing, wooing, and caring for your girlfriend. You cultivated and guarded the relationship. But then you stopped.

No husband would ever articulate this, but the game plan followed by the average husband looks something like this:

Step 1: Find a girl you like.
Step 2: Get that girl to like you back.

THE BAD

Step 3: Impress the girl until she becomes your girlfriend and wants to marry you.
Step 4: Relax.
Step 5: Share a home, bills, conflict, kids, and stress with the girl who was your girlfriend. Don't go anywhere.

MY DAD

My dad did this. After that first blind date when he took my mom out dancing, my dad poured on the heat. He took action, relentless, creative action, to let my mom know that he wanted her and that he would care for her. I grew up hearing the stories.

Shortly after the dancing date, my dad took my mom snow skiing in Lake Tahoe. For the car ride there, my dad prepared a thermos of hot chocolate and hid it behind the driver's seat. After thirty minutes of driving, he pulled out the thermos and passed my mom a steaming cup of hot chocolate. She loved it. After an hour or two of skiing, while they were sitting on the chairlift, my dad surprised my mom by reaching into his pocket and pulling out two Snickers bars. They laughed and ate together. A man in love, my dad continued to pursue and take care of my mom. My mom had never been loved like this. She still tells these dating stories.

After just two months of dating, Ron Buzzard proposed. Joan Miller said yes. And just another two months later, my mom stood before my dad in a white dress and became Joan Buzzard. Ron + Joan = one flesh.

Step 1, check.
Step 2, check.
Step 3, check.

With steps 1, 2, and 3 completed, steps 4 and 5 commenced. Life got busy. Bills came. Kids came. Problems came.

My dad was a truck driver. I used to visit him at the truck yard, and he'd lift me inside the cabs of the big semitrucks with his big, greasy hands so I could pretend that I was driving. One night, when I was a small boy, we returned home from a company Christmas party to find that our home had been robbed. The place was a mess. The thieves took everything. They even took my blue piggy bank. They even took all our Christmas presents under the tree. They even took a pie from our freezer. That night, Ron Buzzard got mad.

My dad was so mad that the next day he decided to quit his job as a truck driver and start his own alarm company. He wanted to protect other people from what had just happened to his family. There was a lot of work to do. My dad learned how to install an alarm system in our home, then he put an ad in the Yellow Pages and started installing alarms in other people's homes. My dad's business, Liberty Bell Alarm, was born. He poured himself into building the business. Liberty Bell Alarm eventually grew from a company of one employee to a company of one hundred employees. My dad did it—he created a successful business that served and protected others.

Meanwhile, the dating stopped. My dad stopped taking my mom out dancing, preparing thermoses of hot chocolate, and passing her surprise Snickers bars. Ron Buzzard worked a lot. He had a business to build. And he had a lot of stress to manage. Joan Buzzard gave birth to two boys—first me, then my younger brother, Mark. My dad's passionate pursuit of the girl he took dancing declined into sharing a home, a new business, bills, two kids, and problems with his wife. Now I don't want to overstate this—Ron and Joan continued to enjoy each other. I have fond memories of watching my parents kiss in the kitchen. But the chase stopped.

THE MISSION

A man needs a mission. Men were created to carry out a mission, and if a man does not have a mission, he feels lost and impotent. We get this from the first man. Immediately after creating Adam, God put him in the garden of Eden and gave him his mission: to work it and keep it. To cultivate and guard. Standing before Adam was a vast garden in need of care, cultivation, and protection. Later, standing before Adam would be a beautiful woman in need of his care, cultivation, and protection. But before Adam found the woman, he experienced a season of being alone. He tended the garden. He worked. He gave names to all the animals and soon realized there was not a suitable companion for him among the beasts and the birds. The search continued. Then one day, God took a rib from Adam's side and fashioned it into a woman. Still aching from the sweet surgery, Adam sees her and he shouts! He can't hold it in; poetry pours from his mouth, and Adam's first recorded words express his extravagant delight in Eve. This is what Adam has been searching for. Adam + Eve = one flesh. Mission accomplished.

The modern man operates as though the mission ends once he's married his woman. The chase is over, he thinks. And since a man must have a mission, men move on to other missions. Men seek new ground to cultivate and guard. Husbands leave their marriages in maintenance mode while they pursue other objectives. This is why my dad poured himself into building a business that would serve and protect other people's homes while stalling his pursuit, service, and protection of the bride who lived in his own home. It's a fundamental misunderstanding of marriage, mission, and manhood.

Men date their girlfriend. And once they marry their girlfriend, they live with a wife they stop dating. Yes, there are wonderful exceptions to this. But those men and those marriages are the exceptions, not the norm. I wrote this book because there are so few of these men. I wrote this book so that what is true of a few men could become true of many men.

Most men think the mission ends after they marry the woman they love, that the most exciting and rewarding work is over. That's because this is how a mission works. A mission has a before and an after. A mission has a starting line and a finish line. Most men think they crossed that finish line a long time ago. The reality is that the mission has only just begun. The reality is that the finish line stands in a land far, far away.

Men:

What if there's more to life than what you're seeing?

What if you have a life-or-death mission on your hands?

What if you looked out across the horizon and saw a far-off finish line that will require your blood, sweat, and tears to cross?

What if a naked woman named Eve lives in your house?

What if your rib is missing and Eve has it?

What if there is more to discover, more to cultivate, and more to guard than you think?

What if your best years of life lie in front of you, not behind you?

THE BAD

What if Ron took Joan out dancing again, and the dance was even better than their first dance?

What if?

WHERE ARE YOU?

"Where are you, Adam?" God is pursuing you with the same question. Adam heard the question after his failure in the garden. My old friend didn't hear the question until he heard the news of the affair. My dad didn't hear the question until he heard the voice of the doctor: "Cancer."

That was ten years ago. Ron learned that Joan had advanced breast cancer. And that's when my dad heard God's voice. "Where are you, Ron?"

The surgeries started. The chemotherapy started. The sickness started. My mom lost her hair. My mom lost her health. My mom lost her old body.

And that's when it started. That's when Ron started taking Joan dancing again.

TAKE ACTION

1. Start dreaming again. What new dreams is God giving you for your marriage?
2. Tell other men how this book is impacting you.
3. Refer to your wife as your "girlfriend" in public settings. She will like this.

PART THREE

THE NEW

6

WHERE MARRIAGES GO *RIGHT*, PART I: THE HUSBAND

Every time a boy is born, we should think of Genesis 2:15. The moment we see the ultrasound picture, the moment we hear the cry of a boy exiting the womb and entering the world, we should recite in our minds:

> The LORD God took the man and put him in the garden of Eden to work it and keep it. (Gen. 2:15)

Boys are born with a mission: to work and keep, to cultivate and guard. God put Adam on the earth, and God pushes boys out of wombs to be cultivators and guardians.

I'm the father of three boys—Cru, Hudson, and Gus. Cru entered the world at 8:00 a.m. on a Thursday morning, a scheduled C-section because he was upside down in his mother's womb. Less than two years later, Hudson arrived on a Sunday afternoon during the fourth quarter of a San Francisco 49ers football game. The Niners won. The night of Hudson's second birthday, Taylor woke me up at 1:00 a.m.

and we raced to the hospital, just in time for the arrival of Gus. All three Buzzard boys were born at the same hospital, delivered by the same doctor. When the doctor presented me with each of my sons, I thought of Genesis 2:15. I thought about the mission God's entrusted to these three men in training. I thought about the twin pillars of their mission: responsibility and power.

RESPONSIBILITY

God gives men enormous responsibility. And the weightiest responsibility he gives to a man is a woman—a wife. In this union, a man's ability to cultivate and guard is put to the greatest test. Will the man lay down his life in order that his wife may flourish? That is the question that measures a marriage. In order for the garden of marriage to be properly cultivated and guarded, a man must give more than he's ever given.

Many men avoid this responsibility. Some men abandon this responsibility. A few men appreciate this responsibility. No man can handle this responsibility.

This is the place to revisit what I said in chapter 3:

It's your fault. This is the second most important truth to learn from this book: it's your fault. You are the husband. You are the man. And God has given man the ability to be the best thing or the worst thing that ever happened to a marriage. Before you can be the best thing that ever happened to your marriage, you must see that you have always been the worst thing that happened to your marriage. If you want to change a marriage, change the man. Why? Because the man is what is wrong, and the man is what, made right, alters the course of everything.

Everybody knows there's something wrong with men. The man problem has been in the news for decades. For decades society has told us that the problem with men is a responsibility problem—that if men acted like men, acted responsibly, things would be better.

I disagree.

Yes, responsibility is part of the problem. The world is full of irresponsible men. Genesis 2:15 gives men a responsibility that is shirked more often than it is embraced. Ephesians 5 further defines this responsibility for husbands: "Husbands, love your wives, as Christ loved the church and gave himself up for her" (Eph. 5:25), a verse many husbands aren't quick to quote or execute. Responsibility is a problem, but it isn't the heart of the problem.

The problem is power.

God gives men a mission. God commissions husbands to cultivate and guard—to date their wives. This mission requires responsibility and power. The problem with men isn't the responsibility, the problem is men think they have the power to carry out the responsibility.

POWER

Men need to be taught about power, not responsibility. I spent the first five chapters of this book talking about responsibility so that I could spend the rest of this book talking about power.

I bought my first car at age sixteen, a silver 1984 Toyota Tercel with one hundred thousand miles on it, an oil leak, and an aftermarket CD player. I loved that car. I kept my football pads in the trunk, and the whole car smelled like football.

One afternoon, my car wouldn't start. I couldn't figure it out. I had plenty of gas. The car had been running great, and I had just checked the oil. I turned the key in the ignition and nothing happened. Then I realized—the battery was dead. No amount of turning the key would do anything. The power source of my engine was dead. I needed outside help.

That afternoon I got my first jump start. I waved down a truck that was passing by. The driver happened to have jumper cables. He pulled his big truck next to my small car, we popped open the hoods of our vehicles, he attached his end of the cables to his fully powered battery, and I attached my end of the cables to my dead battery. He turned on his engine and power started transferring from his truck to my car. Within a few minutes I turned the key in my ignition and, vroom vroom, my car started. I had power again. I thanked the man and drove home.

I think most men are fairly aware of their responsibility as husbands. They know they need to drive the car. But across our world men are sitting in their cars turning the key wondering why nothing is happening. Men don't see that their battery is dead. Men don't see that they need power from the outside, power that comes from someone else, in order to carry out the mission.

I've told you the second-most-important truth to learn from this book: it's your fault—you are the worst thing that ever happened to your marriage. You needed to hear that first. Now let's hear the most important truth: Jesus makes men new—Jesus turns husbands like you and me into the best thing that ever happened to our marriages.

My friend Ed hails from England. We smoke cigars together

and talk about Jesus, life, and our dreams. Taylor and I enjoy going on double dates with Ed and his wife, Nicci. Ed and Nicci have a great marriage. They are a lot of fun, and they sound really smart and godly because of their British accents.

Last year, after ten years of marriage and five years of trying for kids, Nicci discovered she was pregnant with twins. Their excitement was so thick you felt like you could grab onto it and put some of it in your pocket. Ed and Nicci were giving birth to twin boys! The baby showers commenced. Nicci's tummy grew larger.

I arrived at the hospital a few minutes after Joshua died, Ed and Nicci's newborn son. Nicci had gone into early labor. There in the maternity ward at Stanford Hospital, Nicci gave birth to Joshua and, then, to Daniel. Joshua lived sixty-seven minutes outside of the womb. He died in his parents' arms. Meanwhile, Joshua's brother Daniel fought for life in the neonatal intensive care unit, with tubes and wires connected to every part of his body, a body that was the size of my hand. I've never felt so powerless as a pastor as the day I walked into that hospital room and wept with Ed.

A few days later I officiated at Joshua's funeral. I preached with wet eyes. I helped carry Joshua's casket. I startled over the grief Ed and Nicci expressed over a lost son, the hope they carried for a living son, and the faith they exercised in a good and sovereign God. What struck me most from the funeral was Ed and the strength with which Ed loved his wife. Drained of his dreams, drained of sleep, and disoriented by death, Ed was Genesis 2:15 in action—he cared for his wife with power that seemed to come from outside him. It was like jumper cables were attached to him.

There's a saying that Ed learned from his mom. Ed used to quote it to me, and I found myself thinking about the saying as I watched Ed lead his wife through that week of hell. Ed's mom used this saying to teach her son the true nature of responsibility.

Responsibility: My response to his ability.

You crush a man if you only talk to him about responsibility. You empower a man if you talk to him about response-ability—about living life in response to the power and ability of God.

Manhood, husbandry, and Genesis 2:15 were never meant to be carried out in isolation from God. God gave the first man, and God gives us men, a mission that can be completed only through dependence. God doesn't demand men live life on the basis of their own resources; he summons us to live in confident dependence on his resources. He has the power. Our responsibility is to respond to his ability.

Jesus wakes us up to the life we were created to live—a life powered by God, not self. When Jesus gets a hold of a man, he makes a man new. He gives power. Jesus takes men with dead batteries and puts them in relationship with the living God. It's as though men experience Genesis 2:7 all over again:

Then the LORD God formed the man of dust from the ground and breathed into his nostrils the breath of life, and the man became a living creature.

Life feels new. The breath of life, the power and Spirit of God, begins taking over the operating system of a man's life. Trajectories change. Husbands who were stuck begin to move forward, begin to steer their marriage in a new and better direction.

Death does this.[1] Sometimes it takes death to show a man where true power comes from. Sometimes it takes death to make a man come alive to the real mission of manhood and marriage: living life and dating your wife in response to God's ability, not your ability.

Ed received the power long before his son died in his arms. Ed had become a new man many years earlier. But my dad didn't come alive until he heard the doctor's diagnosis: "Your wife has cancer." And my old friend didn't come alive until he heard the bad news: "Your wife's had an affair." It took the news of death for these husbands to hear the news of life: real power comes from outside you, not inside you.

Men carry burdens they were not meant to carry. Like many men, my dad grew up on Simon and Garfunkel, listening to "I Am a Rock":

I am a rock,
I am an island.

And a rock feels no pain;
And an island never cries.[2]

That chorus defines manhood for many men. But all this collapses the day the rock feels pain, the day the island cries. When the battery dies, when a man realizes that he's not a rock, then he's ready to build his life and his marriage on the real Rock. And that Rock is full of power. And that Rock feels pain.

TAKE ACTION

1. Quit your excuses. Don't give God or your wife (or yourself) your excuses anymore. Say sorry. Repent. Ask forgiveness. Own up to your old ways; don't make excuses.[3]
2. Reassess the definition of responsibility that is driving your life.
3. Ask God to make you new.
4. Read the entire New Testament over the next three months, circling the following five words every time you spot them: power, gospel, grace, new, and life.

7

WHERE MARRIAGES GO *RIGHT*, PART II: THE HUSBAND'S GOSPEL

Once upon a time there was a man named Justin. He thought he was a rock. He thought it was up to him to do it all as a man, husband, dad, and pastor. He thought he had the power, strength, and resources to carry out Genesis 2:15 in North America, or at least in Northern California. He dreamed of having the best marriage, the best kids, the best friends, the best ministry, the best life. At age seventeen he left home to accomplish his dreams, to start his mission. He headed to college to play football, get a degree, find a wife, and figure out what's next.

ADAM

One of the two characters I identify with the most in the Bible is Adam. I'm just like Adam. God puts a naked woman in front of me, my Eve, and I shout poetry to God, praising him for the bride he's given me and pledging to take great care of her. But the next day, the Serpent slithers into our garden to speak lies. The Evil One tempts Taylor and me to question God's goodness and live life on the basis of his voice, not God's voice. Instead of standing up to guard the garden and crush the Serpent, I sit in my lawn chair and drink beer.

Satan speaks. We listen. We take the bait and bite the fruit. After sucking on the fruit long enough, we taste the poison. That's what sin is: sugarcoated poison—shiny fruit that tastes good at first but has a rotten core. Satan tempts people with candy that has a hidden pill of poison in the middle. Once my Eve and I taste the poison and see the consequences, God speaks:

> God: "Have you eaten of the tree of which I commanded you not to eat?"

> Adam/Justin: "The woman whom you gave to be with me, she gave me fruit of the tree, and I ate." (Gen. 3:11–12)

Adam went from praising God for the woman to blaming God for the woman. Instead of taking responsibility for what was his fault, Adam blames his wife and blames God for what was his fault. I identify with this guy.

Why did Adam blame instead of apologize? I've been thinking about this question lately. Instead of hiding behind a tree of excuses, why didn't Adam approach God and say, "God, I chose to listen to a snake instead of listening to you. I take full responsibility. I am sorry. I deserve the consequences, yet I beg you to forgive me and spare me. I need your mercy and grace."

If you spent a month living in my house watching me interact with my wife, you could tell I descend from Adam. You'd spot the resemblance. Several times a week I do the same thing

Adam did in the garden. I blame instead of apologize. I excuse my sin instead of claim my sin.

Last night I did it again. Last night Taylor and I had a fight. It wasn't one of those major-league marriage fights; this was a minor-league fight. It was a stupid fight. I started it. We were fighting over how Mother's Day went. After the climax of the fight, as we were headed toward resolution, that's when I started the excuses. My failures were staring me in the face so I started assigning blame. By the time I was done I had assigned blame to Taylor, my mother-in-law, my mom, Hallmark, the infamous Buzzard-family events of Mother's Day 2008, the inconvenience that Taylor's birthday is just six days after Mother's Day, my job, and our third son. So I blamed three moms, one corporation, one historical event, the month of May, my job, and an infant for what was my fault.

Why do I do this? Why do we all do this?

I think it has to do with how men measure themselves.

THE MEASURE OF A MAN

Men are always measuring themselves. You can't hang out with a group of three or more men for more than three minutes without hearing them take measurement of themselves. Listen to what men talk about—their accomplishments, successes, and unique experiences that separate them from others. It doesn't matter if the man is a banker, a plumber, a pastor, a CEO, an artist, an athlete, or unemployed—all men craft a standard of accomplishment by which they measure themselves and measure other men.

Men get this from Genesis 2:15. This behavior stems from

a misunderstanding of the mandate God gave men back in the garden of Eden. God gave Adam and God gave us a mission to accomplish. But God never told Adam and never told us to measure ourselves by the mission. God gave us a different standard of measurement.

The measure of a man is not how successful or unsuccessful a man is at carrying out his mission. The measure of a man is not what he says about himself or what other people say about him. The true measure of a man comes from what God says about him.

Adam didn't believe this. And we don't believe it either.

Adam failed at his mission. He didn't keep Genesis 2:15. He didn't guard his garden and his marriage. That's why Adam hid from God and hid from his wife behind the cover of fig leaves and excuses. Adam found his identity in his ability to perform Genesis 2:15, to successfully cultivate and guard. Having royally failed in his performance, Adam's whole identity was at stake. The measurement didn't look good, so Adam hid, excused, and blamed.

Sound familiar?

Remember what I said in chapter 3, that before God gave Adam a wife, he gave him a job—to cultivate and guard the garden. But here's the really good news: before God gave Adam a job, he gave him an identity. Before God gave Adam a job to do or a mission to accomplish, he gave Adam an identity to embrace. Before God told Adam to do anything, he told Adam who he was—he gave Adam the true way to measure and define himself.

And God saw everything that he had made, and behold, it was *very good*. And there was evening and there was morning, the sixth day. (Gen. 1:31)

Very good! After creating Adam, God looks down upon Adam and declares him very good. This is the living God speaking. This is God declaring what he thinks about Adam. This is Adam's identity. What God says goes. If God says Adam is very good, then this is the voice that defines Adam.

Adam = A man created in the image of God and declared "very good" by God.

Adam's Genesis 2:15 calling was meant to flow out of Adam's Genesis 1:31 identity. God told Adam what he thought about him; he gave Adam his approval—before Adam lifted a finger in the garden. Adam received his God-approved identity before he had a chance to do anything to prove himself. This is what we call grace, or the gospel—the good news of receiving favor from God that we don't deserve or earn. But Adam gets it backward. He didn't listen. Instead of believing, accepting, and living consistently with this God-given identity based on grace, Adam settled for an identity based on works. Adam hid, excused, and blamed in the attempt to reestablish his identity, in the attempt to prove that he was not as guilty and unsuccessful as he looked. Adam settled for a life powered by religion instead of a life powered by the gospel.

This has been the biggest problem of my life. I base my identity on my performance. When I perform well at marriage, fatherhood, my job, cultivating and guarding the garden God has given me, and meeting my goals, I feel good about myself. I'm happy with my measurements. But when I perform poorly in these spheres, I don't feel good about myself. I don't like what the measurements say about me, so I hide, make excuses, and blame it all on Mother's Day.

IDOLATRY

Pride is what drives this. It's disguised pride. It's the worst kind of pride. When I base my identity on my performance instead of on what God says about me, I'm putting myself at the center of my life instead of God. I measure myself instead of letting God measure me. I find my identity in myself, not in God.

Adam did it. I do it. You do it.

The heart of sin is building your identity on yourself instead of on God and his grace. The Bible calls this idolatry. You can't be the husband God wants you to be until you understand the idolatry in your life. Idolatry isn't bowing down to carved statues and dancing around totem poles; idolatry is putting something other than God at the center of your life.

Men are really good at idolatry. Men are really good at twisting the mandate of Genesis 2:15 and building their lives around the things they do rather than the gracious God who created them to do. Take this book as an example. The message of this book is *not* for husbands to start working hard at dating their wives and then to base their identity, marriage, and standing with God on how well they do at dating their wives. That message would only lead to deeper idolatry in a man's life— when a husband is performing well he will be proud of himself; when a husband is performing poorly at dating his wife he will be disgusted with himself. Whether it's good performance or bad performance, both responses are self-centered—both are the result of a man building his identity on what he does, not on the grace of God. Instead, the message of this book invites a man to discover a whole new identity, a whole new center to his life in the gospel of God, and for this new power to enable a man to relate to his wife in a whole new way.[1]

This is what God offered Adam after Adam's failure. Adam ran away from God, but God ran to Adam. Adam invented a game called "hide" and hid behind a tree. But God invented a better game called "hide-and-seek," and found the first husband hiding behind a tree. The first husband failed. And God pursued this sinful, scared, insecure, prideful, excuse-soaked, blame-shifting husband.

God started the reconciliation process by talking to Adam. He asked Adam three questions. The first question is the most important: "Where are you?" (Gen. 3:9). This is an opportunity for Adam to take responsibility, to repent. But as we've seen, this husband doesn't do that. He justified himself with excuses. He attempted to maintain his righteousness, his good record, before God and before his wife. Adam had something to prove.

God listens. Then God curses. God doesn't curse Adam; God curses the Serpent. He curses the one who tempted the first married couple to listen to and live by a voice other than God's. At the heart of God's curse is good news. Speaking to the Serpent, God says:

> I will put enmity between you and the woman,
> and between your offspring and her offspring;

> he shall bruise your head,
>> and you shall bruise his heel. (Gen. 3:15)

THE SECOND ADAM

With these words God promises that life will go on for the first husband and wife. They will not die for their sin. In fact, they will be the givers of life. They will have offspring. From the woman will descend a man who will do what Adam failed to do in the garden—who will crush the Serpent, who will defeat Satan. The rest of the Bible is to be read as a search for the Serpent Crusher, anticipating the arrival of a man who will hold fast to his identity in God, guard the garden, and crush the head of the Serpent. Adam failed to do it. A new and better Adam must do it. And as the gospel-laced curse tells us, the new and better Adam will be wounded in the process. The Serpent Crusher will be bruised as he fights the Serpent. The Rock will feel pain.

After speaking with the hiding husband, God takes the life of an innocent animal and uses the animal's skins to clothe Adam and his wife. Fig leaves and excuses didn't work; the first husband and wife needed a covering for their shame that only God could give them. Husbands need this. We try to manage our sin. The idolatry in our lives drives us to cover up our sin with patchy fig leaves and creative excuses. Our attempts at covering up our nakedness always prove inadequate. Only God can adequately clothe us. Only grace will work.

> And the Lord God made for Adam and for his wife garments of skins and clothed them. (Gen. 3:21)

This is the first sacrifice in Scripture, the first time innocent blood is shed to make atonement for someone else's sin. It's foreshadowing. It's a taste of the promise. It's a glimpse into what the second Adam, the Serpent Crusher, will accomplish. Instead of killing the first husband and wife for their sin, God killed an animal. Instead of letting Adam wander in his nakedness and shame, God made garments for him—God clothed him in clothes that he didn't deserve or earn, clothes that reminded Adam that his sin had been paid for. These garments reminded Adam of where his identity came from. The measure of a man, the identity of a man, is not derived from the things he does or doesn't do. A man is to find his identity in what God says about him: "very good," "forgiven," "clothed in grace."

Many years later a descendant of Adam walked this earth. The son of Adam and the Son of God, fully human and fully God, Jesus came to fulfill the promise. Jesus came to do what Adam couldn't do.

Adam failed in a garden. Jesus succeeded in a garden. In the garden of Eden, Adam failed to keep Genesis 2:15; he failed to guard the garden and guard his wife. But in the garden of Gethsemane, Jesus kept Genesis 2:15. Jesus sweat drops of blood as he prepared to lay down his life to protect his spouse—the church. When Jesus makes vows, he keeps them to the death.

Our Serpent Crusher did his job. He lived a sinless life. He kept Genesis 2:15 and did not listen to the Serpent's voice. The second Adam lived the life that the first Adam should've lived, the life you and I should've lived. Then, Jesus crushed the Serpent. The second Adam's heels were nailed to a cross, and hanging on that cross an innocent life was offered up in place of the guilty. An innocent husband died so that guilty husbands could live and wear new clothes.

And three days after his death, the wounded Serpent Crusher rose from the dead. Life, sin, the Devil, and death couldn't beat Jesus. This is not what the Serpent wanted. God's old promise proved true. The second Adam won. The second Adam went beyond Genesis 2:15. The second Adam did more than carry out his responsibility. He carried out our responsibility.

JESUS MAKES MEN NEW

Jesus took responsibility for what wasn't his fault. Jesus took responsibility for your sin, your mess, your failures.

> Responsibility: My response to his ability.

> Responsibility: My response to the One who took responsibility for my mess.

The Bible calls this message the gospel. The heart of the gospel is that Jesus, the second Adam, took responsibility for what wasn't his fault, offering men a new life driven by a new power.

Jesus doesn't make men better. Jesus makes men new.

That first time I looked at Taylor in that Palo Alto kitchen, my life changed. I fell in love. Everything became new. Looking at Taylor still moves me, but something even greater happens when men look at Jesus.

I thought I saw Jesus clearly a long time ago, but the last few years Jesus has stunned me. Every day he becomes more amazing to me. He is always surprising me. His gospel proves bigger and better with each passing week. Nobody has ever loved me the way Jesus loves me. I deserve none of it. It feels like Jesus has reached into my chest and given me a new heart. The pivot point of my life has changed. I'm not trying so hard to get the world to revolve around me. I feel free.

Men, you will not pursue your wife well until you know the God who pursues you. The Bible is the most romantic book in the world. The Bible, the gospel, is God shouting: "I loved you, but I lost you, and I want you back."[2]

I loved you.

But I lost you.

And I want you back.

Men, no matter the state of our marriages, I want us loving our wives with this heaven-sent passion. But we can't do it until we believe, until we see, that Jesus has first loved us like this. "Husbands, love your wives, as Christ loved the church and gave himself up for her" (Eph. 5:25). He loved us. He lost us. He got us back. He gave himself up for us so that we could give ourselves up for our wives.

Men, what you believe will drive how you live. Every husband has a belief system that drives his life and drives his marriage. Religion destroys men and destroys marriages, but the gospel makes men new and makes marriages new. Will you believe, whether for the first time or for the thousandth time, what the second Adam has done for Adams like us?

Yes, Adam is one of the two characters I identify with the most in the Bible. But I identify with the second Adam more. I've realized I can't live life and love my wife through the power of my own resources and righteousness. It's not enough. I screw everything up. I need the help, power, and grace of Jesus—the One who took responsibility for my mess. My responsibility is to respond to his ability. And my identity as a man comes from what he's done for me and what he says about me, not from what I've done or from what others say about me. The gospel has made me a new man.

TAKE ACTION

1. Read Genesis chapter 3 with your wife. Talk together about the dynamics of sin, temptation, and grace at work in this chapter and how you see them play out in your marriage.
2. Detect and name the idols that tend to drive your life. (Power? Control? Comfort? Approval?) Read a good book on idolatry and the gospel, such as Timothy Keller's *Counterfeit Gods: The Empty Promises of Money, Sex, and Power, and the Only Hope That Matters* (Dutton, 2009).
3. Believe the gospel.

8

WHERE MARRIAGES GO *RIGHT*, PART III: THE HUSBAND'S ACTION

Taylor's parents divorced shortly after her first birthday. Both of her parents remarried shortly after her third birthday. Taylor spent the first ten years of her life here in the Silicon Valley, living with her mom and stepdad and visiting her dad and stepmom, who lived a few miles up the road. She doesn't have a single memory of her mom and dad being married.

Shortly after Taylor's tenth birthday, she moved to Boston with her mom and stepdad. It was summertime. A fellow incoming fifth grader invited Taylor to a weeklong summer camp on a lake in New Hampshire. Taylor wanted to go because she wanted friends; she'd just left everything familiar and fond to her three thousand miles away in California. Taylor's mom and stepdad said yes. They helped her pack her bags for a week of summer camp.

Taylor arrived at Lake Winnipesaukee. She and her friend received their cabin assignment and started settling in, making new friends, and exploring camp. The embarrassing stutter Taylor had developed from the stress of family life and the cross-country move started to fade as Taylor relaxed. She felt at home here. Here, Taylor's life was forever changed.

A few days into camp, Taylor discovered this was a Christian camp. A few days into camp, Taylor heard a message that changed everything. She heard the gospel. For the first time, Taylor was told the only story that could make sense of her story: Jesus came to earth to forgive your sin, redeem the pain and mess in your life, and give you a relationship more important than any earthly relationship, a relationship with God—a relationship so close you can call God "Father." It sounded too good to be true. It sounded too good not to be true. Taylor believed. Under that New Hampshire sky, a miracle happened. Taylor was born again. Ten-year-old Taylor received new life.

Back in California, Taylor's dad and stepmom had been praying for this. They were ripped apart that Taylor now lived so far away. So they did what they could. They prayed. They prayed for nothing to stand in the way of Taylor knowing God. Back in California, I was praying for the same thing. I was only eleven at the time, but my mom and I were still praying for my future wife—praying for her to know Jesus and for God's hand of protection to be on her life. Little did I know what God was doing with a girl named Taylor on the East Coast.

Having placed her faith in Jesus, ten-year-old Taylor received a new identity, a new record, a new power, and a new future. Life would never feel the same again.

A NEW IDENTITY

The gospel gives men and women a new identity. Before meeting Jesus, Taylor felt like an orphan. She had parents (four of them), but Taylor still felt like an orphan. An orphan is someone who doesn't have the security of parents, who feels alone and afraid. Ever since the sin of the first husband and wife, the Bible teaches that everyone is born into this world wonderfully fashioned in the image of God, yet also with the heart of an orphan—a hard heart prone to acting independently of God and running its own life rather than trusting a loving Father to guide its life. Because of the ways she had sinned and the ways she had been sinned against, Taylor viewed herself as an orphan. This identity drove her life.

But at that summer camp, the gospel replaced Taylor's old identity with a new identity. Taylor was told that through the work of Jesus, God turns hard-hearted orphans into soft-hearted sons and daughters. For the first time, Taylor saw herself as a daughter. She understood that she was now God's child, the beloved daughter of her heavenly Father.

> And I will be a father to you,
>   and you shall be sons and daughters to me,
> says the Lord Almighty. (2 Cor. 6:18)

A NEW RECORD

The gospel also gives men and women a new record. Just like the first husband and wife, we are good at hiding our record. We hide the account of the good and bad things we have done. We know our record isn't what it should be. We hide behind fig leaves and excuses, not wanting God or anybody else to know about our imperfect record, our guilt, and our shame. We even hide from ourselves, not wanting to take an honest look at our own report card.

At camp Taylor learned about God's holiness—his perfect record of righteousness—and learned that a perfect God cannot be in relationship with a guilty and imperfect human. Though she hadn't lived a lot of life yet, Taylor knew her record wasn't good enough. She wished she could fix it. Then she heard the gospel and learned that Jesus had already fixed her record. Taylor heard that Jesus lived the life she should've lived, a life with a perfectly sinless record; and that Jesus died the death she should've died, absorbing the penalty for an imperfect record. Taylor learned that Jesus exchanged records with her—that the second Adam's life and death gave her a record of forgiven guilt and perfect righteousness to present to God. Taylor rejoiced over this new record! Now she stood before God with an A+ that Jesus had earned for her. God viewed Taylor just as if she'd never sinned and just as if she'd always obeyed. She didn't have to hide anymore. Now she had a new record that she could never lose.

> And you, who were dead in your trespasses . . . God made alive together with him [Jesus], having forgiven us all our trespasses, by canceling the record of debt that stood against us with its legal demands. This he set aside, nailing it to the cross. (Col. 2:13–14)

A NEW POWER

The gospel doesn't just give you a new identity and a new record, it also gives you a new power. We desperately need this new power. Like everybody else on the planet, my wife was born into this world with a heart quick to chain itself to slave masters—to idols, to false gods who promise salvation and satisfaction but only deliver slavery and dissatisfaction. At an early age, Taylor latched onto approval, thinking earning others' approval would grant her the love and the life she deeply desired. Two decades later, this idol can still hold sway in my wife's life. At an early age, I latched onto control, believing that if I could control my life and my world, everything would be okay. And, just like Taylor, this idol can still hold sway in my life. But it doesn't have to.

Jesus doesn't just rescue us from the *penalty* of sin, he also rescues us from the *power* of sin. Taylor received this power at her conversion at summer camp. There at camp, the Holy Spirit—the third member of the Trinity—God himself, rushed upon Taylor and began to dwell inside Taylor. The Spirit of God began to live inside a skinny, chicken-legged, ten-year-old female body. Having placed her faith in Jesus and Jesus having placed his Spirit inside Taylor, Taylor now navigated life with a new power. The power of sin, the constant lure of approval, began to shrivel in Taylor's life. She no longer felt so powerless, powerless to do the good and right things she wanted to do. She now found herself power-full, full of the power of the Holy Spirit driving and directing her new life.

> But you will receive power when the Holy Spirit has come upon you. (Acts 1:8)

> For I am not ashamed of the gospel, for it is the power of God for salvation to everyone who believes. (Rom. 1:16)

A NEW FUTURE

The gospel makes everything new. It not only gives men and women a new identity, record, and power, but it also gives us a new future. In order to live, you need hope. People die on the inside when they lose hope, when they can't see a better future. Headed to camp, Taylor didn't see a bright future. For her, the future looked like following the American Dream, a dream that Taylor already knew was empty. The American Dream, the American story, looks like this:

> Birth ➔ School ➔ College ➔ Starter Job ➔ Starter Marriage ➔ Picket Fence ➔ 2.5 Kids ➔ Divorce ➔ Second Marriage ➔ Steady Job ➔ Dump Kids ➔ Retire to Florida ➔ Death[1]

Taylor didn't want this. She was scared about the future. But at camp, she received a new future. She learned that when Jesus breaks into your life, the future looks new. Taylor learned that she didn't have to follow the American story; she was now part of God's story. It was like discovering a new and enchanted country in your backyard that you never knew existed. Taylor discovered that God was in control of the universe and the number of hairs on her head, that her Father was leading her forward into a good future of love, joy, and grace. She learned that her Father would take all the hard, bad, and painful things that happen in life and turn them into something beautiful. She learned that death wasn't the end, that Jesus beat death, and that on the other side of death stands a forever future of passionate living in the presence of God and his people, a future that gets better with each passing day.

If God is for us, who can be against us? He who did not spare his own Son but gave him up for us all, how will he not also with him graciously give us all things? (Rom. 8:31–32)

BAPTIZING MY WIFE

Taylor returned from camp a new person, but the environment back home hadn't changed. Taylor didn't have a home, a church, or friends to nurture her new faith, so the growth was slow. "Baby steps" is the phrase Taylor used on our first date to describe what her relationship with God looked like from ages ten to twenty. But during that decade Taylor kept her Bible by her bedside. On certain late nights she read that Bible and heard her Father talking to her. And Taylor would talk back to her Father, pouring her heart out to him. And I continued praying for a bride I hadn't yet met.

During her sophomore year of college at Georgetown, Taylor experienced a revival in her relationship with God. The reality of the gospel—the new identity, record, power, and future she had been given once again took her breath away. For the first time, Taylor was part of a church community, and her faith flourished. After Taylor graduated, she spent the summer working as a camp counselor at the place where it all started— the old camp on Lake Winnipesaukee. Under that same New Hampshire sky, twenty-two-year-old Taylor told ten-year-old girls the good news of the gospel. She watched miracles happen as God transformed many lives that summer. Taylor had come full circle. But there was still one more circle to complete.

After summer camp ended, Taylor moved to San Francisco. She wanted to be back in the Bay Area, close to her roots, her dad and her stepmom. Taylor moved into a San Francisco apartment with a girlfriend from college and started looking for work. She wanted to pursue her career and did not want to pursue anything related to marriage. She had seen too much divorce. Taylor thought she might consider marriage in her late thirties or early forties, in twenty or so years, once she was more sure of herself and more sure that a marriage would last. God had other plans. Taylor and I met two weeks after she moved to the Bay Area. Six months later I proposed. And three months after that, four hundred people gathered to watch Taylor wear a white dress and exchange vows with me in a church a mile down the street from where Taylor's mom and dad were married. You should've been there. My mom even spoke at the wedding, telling the story of the bedside prayers we used to pray for my bride.

Dating Taylor was like taming a wild stallion. It was hard work and it was a lot of fun. It still feels that way.

When I think about what it means for me to date my wife, I think about Taylor's baptism. Shortly after I proposed to Taylor, I got to baptize Taylor. Though she'd become a follower of Jesus many years earlier, Taylor had never been taught about baptism. So one Sunday afternoon, family and friends from our church gathered at a creek in a redwood forest near where she lived. Taylor wore a white dress. A fellow pastor and I took Taylor by the hand and baptized her in the cold creek, in the name of the Father, the Son, and the Holy Spirit.

As Taylor came up from the water, something happened. The only way I can explain it is that as I lifted my wet girlfriend out of the water, God opened up my eyes to see more than I'd seen before. The gospel struck me in a fresh way. I saw, I felt, that Jesus really does make people new. It hit me that Taylor belonged to God, and so did I, and that nothing could change that reality. It hit me that baptized Taylor stood before God and I stood before God with a perfect record, despite our pasts and despite the screwups that were sure to come in the future. It hit me that the Spirit of God really did live inside my fiancée and inside me, and that this somehow changes everything. It hit me that a bright new future stretched out in front of us, a future of God making all sad things come untrue. Then and there I decided that our relationship needed to be defined, directed, and driven by this revolutionary gospel.

I think I date my wife well. I think I'm a good husband. So does Taylor and so do people who know us and know our marriage. I don't have any secrets or special tricks. My only secret is that I feel deep in my guts that God has given me a life and a wife that I don't deserve. Grace is my secret.

That's why when I think of dating my wife, I think of Taylor's baptism. I view dating Taylor—cultivating and guarding Taylor—as the process of reminding her of what I saw at her baptism: Jesus changes everything. This is when a marriage gets electric. When a husband's belief system is overtaken by grace, he will act toward his wife in a new way, in a way that reminds his wife of grace. When this happens, the entire culture of a marriage begins to change.

Old idols lose their power.

Old habits die.

Old hurts are forgotten.[2]

Old guilt disappears.

THE NEW

Old fears fade.

Hope shows up.

A man and a woman begin to dream again.

Things feel new.

TAKE ACTION

1. Ask God to give you his heart for your wife. Ask God to give you a fresh crush on your wife.

2. Keep reminding yourself that the culture of your marriage can change. Things don't have to stay the way they are. Make a list of all the ways you are convicted and convinced your marriage needs to change.[3] Ask the Holy Spirit to guide you in this.

3. Pray for the power of the gospel to show up in your life and in your marriage in a fresh, new way.

4. Remember that Satan hates marriages. You have a supernatural enemy who hates you and hates your marriage. Know your enemy and decide to fight back.[4]

9

A NEW DREAM FOR YOUR MARRIAGE

There is one right way to respond to God's grace: with faith and a new dream. For the gospel to be a real power in your life and in your marriage, you must respond to it with faith—you must believe it. This isn't something you do once; this is something you do daily. Being born again, becoming a new man by the power of God's Spirit, is a miracle that happens only once. But every day we face the opportunity to either rebelieve and live consistent with the miracle of grace or stay stuck in the mud of old ways. Because Jesus changes everything, every day we face the opportunity to pursue a new dream—a new vision for what life and marriage can look like.

Nothing happens without a dream.

Think about it. Think about any great accomplishment in world history—a big dream drove the accomplishment. Brave-hearted William Wallace defeated the English army with a small band of Scotsmen because he dreamed of a better future for Scotland. Charles Lindbergh completed the first nonstop flight from New York to Paris because he dreamed that he could do what no one else had done. Martin Luther King Jr. faced extraordinary odds and violent opposition to lead the Civil

Rights Movement and to bring new freedom to America. Why? Because he had a dream.

DREAM BIG

Husbands should be big dreamers.

Men, you should have a bigger dream for your marriage than your wife has for your marriage. You are the leader of your marriage. And men, you should have a bigger dream for your marriage than you have for your work or any other responsibility or interest in your life. Next to your relationship with Jesus, your biggest dream should revolve around how to steward the marriage God has given you—how to best cultivate and guard the wife God has entrusted to you.

One of my favorite married couples is Nick and Sue Lombardo.[1] I met Nick and Sue when I was a twenty-three-year-old waiter living in Santa Barbara visiting the Silicon Valley to interview for a job as a youth pastor. Meeting Nick and Sue was a big factor in accepting the job—I wanted to spend more time around this husband and wife. Little did I know that nine months after meeting the Lombardos, I would meet Taylor, and the Lombardos would mentor us through our dating and the first few years of our marriage.

Nick and Sue were high-school sweethearts—they met when Nick was seventeen and Sue was fifteen. They married two years later. Last month Nick and Sue returned from a trip to Italy to celebrate Nick's eightieth birthday and their sixtieth wedding anniversary. For sixty years Nick and Sue have been happily married. For sixty years Nick has been dating his wife. For sixty years Nick and Sue have been best friends.

Nick and Sue live in a beautiful home on several acres in the Santa Cruz Mountains at the end of the steepest road I've ever driven on. Forty years ago Nick built this home with his own hands, working at IBM during the day and working on his home at night. We love going to Nick and Sue's house. Last winter I took my three sons with me to cut down our Christmas tree on Nick's property. With saws in our hands, Nick, my two older boys, and I hiked down a steep slope in the middle of a rainstorm and cut down an eight-foot-tall tree that stands as the best Christmas tree we've ever had. Nick is one of the few men I know who I tell my sons I want them to grow up to be like.

Taylor and I will never forget one afternoon we spent with the Lombardos. Gathered around the fireplace in the Lombardos' living room, the four of us had a long talk about sex, marriage, friendship, and leaving a legacy. I don't know how we started talking about sex, but we did. Taylor and I were newly married at the time and as we talked about the excitement of sex in a new marriage, Nick and Sue laughed at us. They looked us straight in the eye and told us that sex gets better with each decade of marriage. They told us that their sex life in their late seventies was far better than their sex life in their early twenties. They shared that with each decade they grew to love each other more, enjoy their friendship more, and make love to each other better than before. As two virgins just now discovering the thrilling new territory of sex and marriage, Taylor and I stared at Nick and Sue in disbelief. I tried picturing what it would look like to make love to my wife when we're eighty years old and covered in wrinkles.

I didn't get it then. I get it now. A good marriage is like a good wine—it gets better with age. Give a good marriage time, and the sex, the love, the friendship, the joy, and the dating get better. Maturity happens. Many men settle for one-night stands when they could have every-night stands with a loving and faithful bride/best friend, stands that get better with each passing month, year, and decade.

Nick taught me how to dream big for my marriage. That afternoon in their living room, Nick talked about the dream he entered marriage with: to take great care of Sue and pass on a legacy of following Jesus. Nick's dream has been accomplished. Seventy-eight-year-old Sue is a happy, happy wife who has flourished for sixty years under Nick's care and protection. A few weeks ago I bumped into the Lombardos while they were on a date. Nick had his right hand on the small of Sue's back and used his left hand to open the door for Sue as he walked her into one of their favorite Italian restaurants. They'd just returned from their anniversary trip to Italy the night before, so they began telling me stories from their trip. They told me the latest updates on their family members who accompanied them on the trip, updates on their three children, ten grandchildren, and seven great-grandchildren—the majority of whom are following Jesus. That's a legacy.

It all started with a date and a dream. A seventeen-year-old boy named Nick took a fifteen-year-old girl named Sue on a date. He had a dream—a dream to marry her, to take great care of her, and to pass on a legacy of following Jesus. I never knew the teenage Nick; I've only known Nick in his seventies, and now, his eighties. Nick is one of my heroes. He's never stopped dating his wife. What he started at age seventeen, he's in the process of finishing at age eighty. We need more husbands like Nick, men who finish what they start.

DREAM NEW

The most rebellious, countercultural thing you can do in our culture is to be happily married until death do you part. Very few people are doing it. Men, the most rebellious, countercultural thing we can do in our culture is to be men like Nick.

Nick isn't perfect and Nick's marriage isn't perfect; it's simply a marriage where the power of the gospel has been alive and active for sixty years. It's a marriage where the man has been doing his job, Genesis 2:15—cultivating and guarding—responding to the ability of God, for sixty years. This has made their marriage the healthiest and happiest marriage I know.

Marriages like this are rare. Men like this are rare. But things don't have to stay this way. We can have better men and better marriages.

Jesus changed Nick's life a long time ago, allowing Nick to enter marriage with a grace-powered dream that has driven his marriage for sixty years. Most men don't start marriage this way. Most men need someone to yell at them and tell them to dream a new dream for their life and their marriage.

This was the case for the first husband. After Adam's great failure in the garden, God pursued Adam, forgave Adam, and gave Adam permission to dream again—to live life on the basis of God's grace and power, not on the basis of past failures. Adam did it. Adam responded to God's surprising grace with faith and a new dream.

After embracing God's words of grace, the first thing the first husband did was name his wife.

> The man called his wife's name Eve, because she was the mother of all living. (Gen. 3:20)

Until this point, Adam's wife didn't have a name. Now, after their greatest failure in marriage and in relationship with God, Adam names his wife Eve. Eve means "life" or "life giver." Instead of believing that their sin and past choices doomed them to death, Adam chose to believe in God's grace—that new life was ahead for their marriage. He believed that the Savior of the world would descend from his lineage. He took God at his word and believed the future could look new.

The first husband believed the gospel.

The first husband named his wife—Life.

The first husband began to dream a new dream for his life and his marriage.

Men, dream big and dream new. God's grace is more amazing and more powerful than you think. Take Jesus at his word and dream of what it would look like for your marriage to be founded on God's grace like never before. I've watched good, bad, and average marriages experience revival because the husband encountered God's grace in fresh ways and began to dream again. Keeping a big, new dream out in front of a marriage can perpetually lift a marriage into exciting, new territory.

Men, what's your dream for your marriage? Nick had a dream. What's your dream?

I know of a bad marriage that became a good marriage after

a husband bought his wife a new wedding ring and said he was sorry for years of sexual sin, that from now on their marriage would be new, and that the new ring was a symbol of the new things to come. He had started dreaming about the next ten years looking different from the past ten years.

I know of an average marriage that became a great marriage after the husband began dreaming of what it would look like for him to actually lead his marriage instead of letting it go in whatever direction the wind blew.

I know of a good marriage that became a great marriage after the husband started dreaming of what it would look like for grace to be not just a doctrine in his head, but a power in his life as he related to and loved his wife.

Nothing happens without a dream. Without vision, without a dream, a man and his marriage will stay stuck. But with a dream, a marriage can soar.

Men, respond to God's grace with faith, then dream big.

TAKE ACTION

1. Write down a big, new dream for your marriage. Take a few days to think, pray, and dream, then write out your dream on one sheet of paper. Try to keep your dream concrete, simple, and measurable. Nick's dream was big, yet short and simple: to take great care of Sue and leave a legacy of following Jesus.
2. Study your wife. She's not the exact same woman you married years ago; she has changed and developed. Study what makes your wife tick and make sure you factor your findings into your dream.
3. Take your wife on a date and share your dream with her.
4. Start living the dream.

10

HOW TO DATE YOUR WIFE: DEVELOP THE AIR WAR

On August 16, 2003, I made a promise. In a church packed with family and friends, I looked my best friend in the eye and, holding her hand, I spoke these vows:

> I, Justin, take you, Taylor, to be my wife; and I promise, before God and these witnesses, to be your loving and faithful husband.
>
> First and foremost, I vow to glorify God by pursuing my life and joy in him.
>
> I vow to follow Jesus's model and lay down my life for you.
>
> I vow to put your needs before my own.
>
> I vow to pursue what is best for you.
>
> I vow to be a humble, strong, wise, and patient communicator.
>
> I vow to lead our union with strength, courage, truth, and passion.
>
> I vow to appreciate you, fight for you, and protect you.
>
> In plenty and in want; in joy and in sorrow; in sickness and in health; as long as we both shall live.

I had carefully prepared these vows. I intended to keep them. This was the biggest commitment I'd ever made. I can still feel the slippery sweat sliding between our held hands as I spoke these words. Next, Taylor looked me in the eye and spoke her vows:

> I, Taylor, take you, Justin, to be my husband; and I promise, before God and these witnesses, to be your loving and faithful wife.
>
> I vow to love the Lord our God will all my heart, with all my soul, with all my mind, and with all my strength.
>
> I vow to praise Jesus throughout my life for his generosity in giving you to me as my lifelong partner in adventurous love.
>
> I vow to honor you with my words, my actions, my thoughts, and my heart.
>
> I vow to grip your hand strongly and affectionately.
>
> I vow to turn my heart inside out and offer you full exposure to all that it contains. Never will I hide, always will I sprint to you.
>
> I vow to confess, grieve, feel your pain, and vigorously work toward a deeper selflessness when I fail to love you well.
>
> I vow to love you with freedom and abandon, with laughter and sweetness, with energy and passion.
>
> In plenty and in want; in joy and in sorrow; in sickness and in health; as long as we both shall live.

A crowd of four hundred people listened to us make our promises. My brother stood next to me as my best man. My mom and dad sat in the front row. Taylor's dad and stepmom also sat in the front row next to Taylor's mom and a man whom I'd just met the day before, a man who has become a favorite relative of mine: my Jewish-South-African-ex-stepfather-in-law. (Taylor's mom and stepdad had divorced several years earlier, and her stepdad had returned to live in his hometown in South Africa; he flew in just in time for the wedding.)

Every day I'm reminded of this scene. Hanging on the wall in our home is a large black-and-white picture of what I've just described: Taylor in her white dress, me in my tuxedo, and the crowd listening to our vows. Under the picture sit our handwritten vows, and the rest of the frame is taken up with the signatures and well wishes of everyone who witnessed our wedding. Looking at this picture reminds me of what I've promised. It reminds me of my daily need for God's help and power to keep my promise. It reminds me of the dream I have for my marriage. It reminds me to plan.

HAVE A PLAN

It's one thing to speak vows; it's another thing to keep vows. It's one thing to dream big about your marriage; it's another thing to pursue and implement that dream. A dream drives a marriage, and a plan cements the new realities you want to see in your marriage. To date your wife, you have to plan to date your wife. A ship without a sail and a rudder set in a deliberate direction will never make it to the other shore—it will simply drift at sea. A plan for how to date your wife is your sail and rudder—it will take you to your desired shore.

I know men who have pages and pages of plans for their businesses, their finances, and their hobbies but have never written down a single sentence of planning for their marriage.[1] Vows, dreams, ideas, and good intentions aren't enough. A man needs to plan. You need more than passion to lead your marriage into new territory; you also need a practical plan. Once a man recovers a God-given, gospel-powered dream for his marriage, I encourage him to view his marriage in one-year chunks and to draft an annual plan for how he will date his wife.

PLAN FOR THE AIR WAR AND THE GROUND WAR

Drafting an annual plan for dating your wife starts with the "air war" of your marriage—this is planning for when your B-52 bombers will fly overhead to drop major artillery and troops in support of your marriage, helping you push your marriage forward in significant ways. In the next chapter we'll color in the annual plan by looking at the "ground war" of your marriage— the daily and weekly work on the ground and in the trenches that often goes unnoticed but makes a big difference in the long haul.

I often sit down with men to help them craft an annual plan for their marriages. I've found that most men need help getting started in the practical planning department. Men are comfortable planning in detail for their careers, their upcoming fishing trips, or their new fitness goals because they've been taught to do so. Most men have simply never been taught about the importance of, or a method for, dating their wife. After spending forty-five minutes helping a fellow husband create an annual Date-Your-Wife Plan, I've discovered that this is the first and last time a husband needs help from me.[2] Once a man has been coached through crafting an annual plan and starts implementing it, he feels confident and equipped to continue this habit on his own and create a fresh Date-Your-Wife Plan each year.

There is no one right way to do this. Every marriage is different. Every wife is different. You need to create an annual plan that's unique to the dream God has given you for your marriage and your wife. To help jump-start your own creativity and planning, two samples of annual Date-Your-Wife Plans follow. Remember, right now we're creating the air war portion of the plan. In the next chapter we'll add more color to the plan by creating the ground war.

Every marriage operates on a different calendar. Some men craft plans that follow the calendar year—January through December. Other men craft plans that pivot on their anniversary date. The plan Taylor and I follow is in sync with our anniversary (August 16) and the academic calendar. This works well for us since we have three kids that will soon be in school, and since I'm a pastor my work tracks with the academic calendar. This puts our marriage, our kids, and my work on the same planning timetable—August through July. Because I've seen the August-through-July calendar work well for many marriages, I've used this calendar for both sample plans.

AIR WAR SAMPLE PLAN 1: FIRST YEARS OF MARRIAGE OR EMPTY-NEST YEARS OF MARRIAGE

Below is a simple outline of a Date-Your-Wife Plan that I've seen work well for both newly married and empty-nest couples. This is a sample plan of a newly married couple in the Bay Area, so the locations are specific to the Bay Area, and the goals are specific to a newlywed couple wanting to build a strong foundation by getting regular time together away from the stress and routine of daily life.

Air War Goals

Enjoy a "twelve-month honeymoon." Once a month get out of town for two nights to date my wife, cultivate our friendship, grow our romance, have fun, and relax. Because of our tight newlywed budget, this will be done in the most cost-effective and creative manner possible.[3] Instead of spending money throughout the month on meals out, entertainment, and other items such as expensive coffee drinks, we will save that money and use it toward our monthly getaways. I will use these monthly getaways to love my wife, laugh with my wife, get to know my wife, pray with my wife, and make love to my wife with the intention that these monthly getaways help set the tone for our marriage each month.

August
Two days of wine tasting and relaxing in Napa. Cost: $300 (hotel, a few meals out, wine tasting, and gas).

September
Two-night backpacking trip in Yosemite. Cost: $100 (backpacking, food, and gas).

October
Two-night house swap with friends in San Francisco. Cost: $75 (two meals out).

November
Two-night camping trip in Big Sur. Cost: $75 (campsite and food).

December
Two days relaxing and snowshoeing in Lake Tahoe at a friend's cabin. Cost: $150 (snowshoe rental, food, gas).

January
Two nights car camping and exploring the coast. Cost: $100 (gas and food).

February
Two nights at a bed-and-breakfast in Carmel. Cost: $250 (bed-and-breakfast and two meals out).

March
Two night house swap with friends in San Jose. Cost: $75 (meals out).

April
Two nights at a bed and breakfast in Half Moon Bay. Cost: $200 (bed and breakfast and meals out).

May
Two-night backpacking trip in Yosemite. Cost: $100 (backpacking, food, and gas).

June
Two-night house swap with friends in San Francisco. Cost: $50 (one meal out).

July
Two days relaxing on the beach in Santa Cruz. Cost: $200 (hotel and food).

Total Annual Cost: $1,725.
Cost of Not Doing This: ?

AIR WAR SAMPLE PLAN 2: MARRIED WITH THREE KIDS

Below is the Date-Your-Wife Plan that I've created for Taylor and me for this year of our marriage—our eighth year. Our life is very full right now with three young kids and the pressure and busyness of church planting, plus we're on a tight budget. So this plan is reflective of our station in life and how God is leading me to lead our marriage this year.

Air War Goals

Take great care of Taylor and our marriage in the midst of a busy, demanding, and unpredictable year. Enjoy a weekly date night every Friday night from 8:00 p.m.–10:00 p.m.; twice a month go out for our date and twice a month hold these dates at home. Use these dates to laugh a lot with Taylor and do a big picture check-in on our lives and marriage. Secure free babysitting from friends in our church. Once a month watch the kids and give Taylor a night out with her girlfriends. Once a year take Taylor on a three-night getaway without the kids. Once a year take the whole family on a long vacation with our extended family, utilizing their help in caring for our kids and helping pay for the vacation. This year make it my main focus to build a stronger culture of grace in our marriage. The most practical way I can do this is to criticize Taylor less and encourage Taylor more. Anytime I'm traveling, get one or two people to help Taylor and give her a break from the kids.

August
Friday date night (first and third week: go out; second and fourth week: at home). Cost: $50.
Wife's night out (second Saturday of the month). Cost: $15.

September
Friday date night (first and third week: go out; second and fourth week: at home). Cost: $50.
Wife's night out (second Saturday of the month). Cost: $15.
Throughout football season, order in pizza and watch *Monday Night Football* with my sons while Taylor gets some time to herself.

October
Friday date night (first and third week: go out; second and fourth week: at home). Cost: $50.
Wife's night out (second Saturday of the month). Cost: $15.
Throughout football season, order in pizza and watch *Monday Night Football* with my sons while Taylor gets some time to herself.
Help Taylor throw a combined birthday party for all three of our sons.

November
Friday date night (first and third week: go out; second and fourth week: at home). Cost: $50.
Wife's night out (second Saturday of the month). Cost: $15.
Throughout football season, order in pizza and watch *Monday Night Football* with my sons while Taylor gets some time to herself.
Three-night getaway with my bride, without the kids. Cost: $400.

December
Friday date night (first and third week: go out; second and fourth week: at home). Cost: $50.
Wife's night out (second Saturday of the month). Cost: $15.
Throughout football season, order in pizza and watch *Monday Night Football* with my sons while Taylor gets some time to herself.

January
Friday date night (first and third week: go out; second and fourth week: at home). Cost: $50.
Wife's night out (second Saturday of the month). Cost: $15.

February
Friday date night (first and third week: go out; second and fourth week: at home). Cost: $50.
Wife's night out (second Saturday of the month). Cost: $15.

March
Friday date night (first and third week: go out; second and fourth week: at home). Cost: $50.
Taylor takes a 48 hour personal retreat while I watch the boys. Cost: $300.

April
Friday date night (first and third week: go out; second and fourth week: at home). Cost: $50.
Wife's night out (second Saturday of the month). Cost: $15.

May
Friday date night (first and third week: go out; second and fourth week: at home). Cost: $50.
Wife's night out (second Saturday of the month). Cost: $15.

Throw a party for Taylor's birthday and make Mother's Day special for her.

June
Friday date night (first and third week: go out; second and fourth week: at home). Cost: $50.
Wife's night out (second Saturday of the month). Cost: $15.

July
Wife's night out (second Saturday of the month). Cost: $15.
Take the whole family on a two-week vacation partially paid for by and involving our extended family. Enjoy having extra help with the kids from our family, give Taylor many breaks throughout the vacation, attempt taking Taylor on a one-night getaway without the kids in the middle of the vacation. Cost: $1,000.

Total Annual Cost: $2,425.
Cost of Not Doing This: ?

GOD'S POWER AND PLAN

Vows aren't automatic. Vows aren't magic. Vows don't keep themselves. Men, it's up to us to keep the vows we spoke to our wives.

Every morning I see that black-and-white picture of our wedding day. Every time I look at that picture I remember the vows I spoke to my wife. I love my wife so much. I always will. Come hell or high water, I'm keeping my vows. Doing so requires God's power and a good plan.

We are seeking to do for our wives what God has already done for us. When we least deserved it, God started a relationship with us and spoke vows of love over us. He began planning his relationship with us long before he created us. Think about it. God has made vows with you that he plans to keep, no matter what. Remember the vows God has made to you, remember the vows you have made to your wife, and come up with a fresh plan for how to keep those vows—how to date your wife. Develop an air war plan for how you will keep your vows and date your wife.

> When I passed by you again and saw you, behold, you were at the age for love, and I spread the corner of my garment over you and covered your nakedness; I made my vow to you and entered into a covenant with you, declares the Lord GOD, and you became mine. (Ezek. 16:8)

TAKE ACTION
1. Create the air war portion of a Date-Your-Wife Plan for the next twelve months of your marriage.
2. Take your wife on a date and reveal your plan. Revise and shape your plan together with your wife as she offers her input and tells you her hopes and dreams for your marriage.
3. Plug your plan into your calendars, and don't let anything else compromise these plans. Schedule and make reservations accordingly.
4. Flirt with your wife.

11

HOW TO DATE YOUR WIFE: DEVELOP THE GROUND WAR

For our one-year anniversary I took Taylor on the ultimate date. I convinced my church to give me the month of August off so that I could take Taylor on a road trip from San Francisco to the Arctic Ocean. I put the mattress and down comforter from our bed in the back of my 4x4 pickup truck. I stocked the truck with food, books, maps, backpacking gear, a video camera, and a big knife. We called our trip "The Journey North."

Leaving San Francisco, we traveled through Oregon, Washington, and then Glacier National Park in Montana. After a near-deadly encounter with grizzly bears while hiking the Highline Trail, we crossed into Canada and drove north, following the backbone of the Canadian Rockies through Alberta, British Columbia, and the Yukon Territories. We'd never seen mountains, rivers, lakes, trees, and animals so big. On the night of our anniversary we crossed the border into Alaska. We ate caribou for dinner and shared a glass of wine on the tailgate of my truck. We spent the rest of the month exploring Alaska—backpacking in Wrangell-St. Elias and Denali National Parks, bathing in rivers, hiking on glaciers, enjoying trail runs in the middle of nowhere, making love in gorgeous places, dreaming about our future, navigating occasional marital conflict, reading good books, meeting new people, sleeping under an Alaskan sky that never turned dark, and driving a four-hundred-mile dirt road just so we could say we set foot in the Arctic Ocean. Along the way we encountered more grizzly bears, bison, bighorn sheep, elk, caribou, and moose than I could ever count, logged over twenty thousand miles on my truck, and made memories that forever mark our marriage. It was the trip of a lifetime.

Air war. Our epic journey through Alaska was part of the air war in our marriage. This once-in-a-lifetime trip made an incredible impact on my wife and on our marriage. But it wasn't enough. The air war isn't enough.

A BALANCED BATTLE PLAN

Many men make the mistake of thinking they can take great care of their wife simply through executing an air war. Men think that if they do a few big things with occasional consistency—take their wife out for a fancy dinner, buy their wife a bouquet of red roses, or take their wife on a big vacation—that they've successfully dated their wife. Wrong. To date your wife well, to cultivate and guard your marriage, you need both an air war and a ground war.

Dating your wife with only an air war is like trying to win World War II without putting troops on the ground where the real action is taking place. Dating your wife with only an air war is like trying to learn French culture by flying over to visit Paris every few years, rather than permanently moving in and calling Paris your home. The real action, the real learning, the real change, the real miracles happen on the ground—in ordinary, daily life.

Cultures don't change overnight; they change slowly and steadily as new ideas and practices spread and gain ground over old ideas and practices. Buildings aren't built overnight. They're built brick by brick, until one day you wake up and see that what started with one brick is now ten stories high.

Men, God is calling us to lead a cultural revolution in our marriages. Some of us have a lot of work ahead of us, while others of us have less work to do. We're all reading this book from different positions—some of us have broken marriages, some of us have mediocre marriages, and some of us have uniquely happy marriages. Whatever our position, we all see change that needs to take place. We all have a war to fight and a wife to date. Let's set up a great air war as we plan to date our wives *and* let's set up a great ground war. Let's take big trips to Alaska (or wherever your wife likes to go), *and* let's build brick by brick—taking one ordinary, messy day at a time to love and date our wives.

I have this thing I do. When I hold hands with Taylor I often squeeze her hand three times. I've told her how to translate these three squeezes. Squeeze one: "I." Squeeze two: "love." Squeeze three: "you." Then she squeezes back four times: "I-love-you-too." This is ground-war-level stuff. This is just one small brick. But if you hold your wife's hand like this several times a week, in forty years you'll have built something strong and beautiful. The bricks add up.

Saying "I love you" adds up.

Giving your wife a break on a busy Monday adds up.

Enjoying a Tuesday night relaxing and talking with your wife adds up.

Taking something off your wife's plate on a stressful Thursday afternoon adds up.

Praying for your wife when she doesn't know it adds up.

Those little kisses in the kitchen add up.

The ground war adds up.

The air war perspective on your marriage is from thirty thousand feet up in the air. This perspective allows you to dream, come up with big plans, and view your marriage in idealistic one-year chunks. You've already put together that part of an annual Date-Your-Wife Plan. The ground war perspective on your marriage is entirely different. You can see only a few feet in front of you: life is messy—full of stress, bills, and dirty dishes. When you think of developing a ground war plan you don't think in terms of twelve months, you think in terms of seven days. A complete Date-Your-Wife Plan includes a ground war plan, a general plan for what Sunday through Saturday looks like for you and your wife. Think of it like two wheels on a bike—you need a front wheel (air war) and a back wheel (ground war) to ride a bike. If you have only one wheel, you won't get very far on the bike.

GROUND WAR SAMPLE PLAN: MARRIED WITH THREE KIDS

Below is the Date-Your-Wife ground war plan that I've created for Taylor and me for this year of our marriage.

Ground War Goals

Take great care of Taylor in the midst of a busy year. Find little ways throughout the week to relieve Taylor, encourage Taylor, and enjoy time with Taylor. Protect every Saturday as a family Sabbath. (For twenty-four hours I don't do any work for the church, Taylor doesn't do any housework, we both turn off our computers and e-mail accounts, and we focus on relaxing and playing together as a family.)[1]

Sunday
Work Day
Put the boys to bed. Enjoy a few hours alone with Taylor once the boys are in bed.[2]

Monday
Work Day
After work, watch the boys for an hour so Taylor can get in a run or some time alone.
Put the boys to bed. Enjoy a few hours alone with Taylor once the boys are in bed.

Tuesday
Work Day
Put the boys to bed. Enjoy a few hours alone with Taylor once the boys are in bed.

Wednesday
Work Day
Neighborhood Group (Every Wednesday night Taylor and I host a group of people from our church and our neighborhood for a night of food, friendship, fun, talking about and applying the Bible to our lives, prayer, and strategizing about how to impact our neighborhood for Jesus.).

Thursday
Work Day
After work, watch the boys for an hour so Taylor can get in a run or some time alone.

Put the boys to bed. Enjoy a few hours alone with Taylor once the boys are in bed.

Friday
Work Day
Date Night

Saturday
Family Sabbath—rest, play, and accomplish nothing.

PUTTING IT ALL TOGETHER

Once you've created your air war and your ground war, you've completed an annual Date-Your-Wife Plan. Now all you do is follow the plan. Since now you've blocked off your year and your weeks to date your wife, you can fill in your calendar with everything else in your life: work, activities with the kids, outings with friends, etc. This process ensures that you approach each new year of life with "date-your-wife eyes," that you keep dating your wife a priority above the other priorities in your life. As you move through life, hundreds of difficulties and distractions will come your way that threaten the plan, but before those difficulties hit, you now have a plan that will help you better navigate those difficulties and stay on course as a husband.

What I've seen guys do is print out a copy of their air war and ground war and keep it with them in their wallets, in their cars, in their Bibles, in a notebook, or on their refrigerators at home. As life gets stressful, guys glance back at their plan, and it helps them stay the course. I don't care what you do. I just care that you have a plan.

Now, don't be a legalist. Some guy out there is reading this chapter thinking that if he creates a Date-Your-Wife Plan, prints it out, signs it, prays through it with his wife, has a group of accountability partners hold him to it, looks at it every morning when he brushes his teeth, sews the plan into his boxer briefs, and executes his plan with precision that his life and marriage will magically improve and he'll finally be satisfied with himself as a husband. Don't be that guy. Instead, believe the gospel, dream big for your marriage, craft a plan that involves some measure of an air war and a ground war, follow the spirit of the plan (not the letter of the plan), and date your wife.

Make it fun.

TAKE ACTION

1. Draft the ground war version of a Date-Your-Wife Plan.
2. Start executing your plan.
3. Have fun.

PART FOUR

THE PERFECT

12

DATE YOUR WIFE
UNTIL DEATH DO YOU PART

My junior year of college I went for a run in the hills of Santa Barbara with my friend Andy. We spent the run talking about a problem we'd both noticed at our college: the men weren't pursuing the women. Guys weren't asking girls on dates. We decided to do something about it.

By mile three of our run, we decided to start what we called "The Dating Revolution" at our college. We decided that the two of us would lead the way in creating a culture shift on our campus. We constructed a simple game plan: Andy and I would start asking women out on dates as often as possible, and we would challenge other guys to do what we were doing. Andy and I came up with a motto that we chose to believe whether or not it was true: "Women want to be with us." We repeatedly told ourselves that women wanted to be with us, and then we started asking women out. It worked. Immediately after our run we walked onto campus and each asked out a woman. Those dates went great. We kept at it. Other men followed our lead. Soon, all across our campus, men were dating women.

THE PERFECT

I wrote this book in order to start a dating revolution in our marriages.

Husbands, date your wife.

Date your wife until death do you part.

DEATH

I'm sitting on a bench in a cemetery a half mile from my home. I walked here to write this last chapter. I've been planning on this since I began writing the book—I want us men to feel the gravity of what's to come.

This cemetery is full of dead husbands and wives. Some of the tombstones go back to the 1700s, quite old for a California cemetery. Here, scores of husbands and wives are buried next to each other. Some of the couples died within a short span of each other, within a few years. Others did not. In front of me sits the shared tombstone of Fred and Edna, a couple separated for thirty-eight years by death.

I can't handle the thought of losing Taylor. My eyes are wet just thinking about it. What would it feel like to lose my bride and my best friend, to lose the one with whom I am one flesh?

Taylor and I pray for a long life together. We pray for a long life for our three boys. We pray that our boys would bury us and that we would never have to bury one of them. We even pray that God would grant us the gift of dying close together—thirty-eight years is a long time. But we can't control these things. These prayers are in God's hands. He will govern the galaxies and govern our lives in his wisdom.

Men, my wife will die and your wife will die. Are we prepared for it? Are we preparing our wives for it? To date your wife, to cultivate and guard this relationship until death do you part, is to prepare your wife for what happens when death happens.

When I was twenty-one I pulled a dead body out of a lake. It was the dead body of a man my age, a twenty-one-year-old named Samson Washington. I didn't know Samson. But after swimming out into the middle of a lake at midnight and discovering, holding, and carrying his dead body to shore, I learned Samson's story. I learned that he had lived a hard and reckless life, but that Jesus had recently changed his life—that grace had melted his heart and that he had become a new man. As I learned Samson's story I found myself smiling, knowing that death in the lake wasn't the end for Samson. Holding his dead body changed my life.

Samson's death taught me that life is short and grace is strong. His death taught me that our life span this side of the grave could be a mere twenty-one years and that God's grace is stronger than our past, stronger than our sin, and stronger than our death. The day after Samson's death I wrote a list of resolutions to live my life by. This short list has gone through some refining over the years, but the nuts and bolts of it remain the same. I have seven of these resolutions. The sixth resolution explains how I approach dating my wife:

> Resolved to love, lead, and have fun with my bride and best friend, Taylor—help her become her future glory-self.[1]

RESURRECTION

My wife will die. She might die before me. But that will not be the end. I will see her again. This resolution anticipates this reality.

The message of the Bible is clear: Jesus is alive. Jesus defeated death. After three days buried in a tomb, the second Adam was raised from the dead. Now, anyone who places their faith in Jesus and his resurrection power will also be raised from the dead. Resurrected from death, they will enjoy God forever in a new world, a garden city[2] that surpasses the original garden of Eden, where there will be no such thing as suffering, sin, death, or tears.

When my wife dies she will become her "future glory-self." Taylor will still be Taylor, but she will be a glorified Taylor. Sin and suffering and shortcomings will no longer mark my wife; she'll be wonderfully free from all of that. Once in a while I catch glimpses of who my wife will become—I see in shadow form what my bride will look like without the scars and the sin of this fallen world. I see her future glory-self.

My exciting calling as a husband is to help Taylor become, to prepare her to become, her future glory-self. Dating your wife is helping your wife become her future glory-self.

THE GOOD. THE BAD. THE NEW. THE PERFECT.

This book has followed a fourfold structure: the good, the bad, the new, and the perfect. This is the fourfold story line of the Bible and of our marriages.

Things start out good. Relationships are intact, secure, and exciting. Then things go bad. We sin, we screw up, we hurt, and we get hurt. We cry out for help. Then God hears, and God shows up. Grace happens. Jesus comes to us, forgives us, and makes things new. And eventually, everything becomes perfect.

Life in Eden was good, but it was never perfect. Heaven

and earth were still separate places. God and man did not dwell together. But where the story eventually takes us is to a time and a place where heaven and earth meet, where what God has begun to make new will be made perfect.

My wife will be there. I will be there. And though I don't know how marriage will operate in heaven,[3] I believe whatever Taylor and I experience then and there will be infinitely better than what we share here and now. Anything good in our marriage right now is a result of the presence of Jesus in our relationship. On the other side of the grave, Taylor and I will have some kind of a relationship that involves a lot more of the presence of Jesus. We will have some kind of a relationship that involves our future glory-selves. We won't fight. We won't sin against or hurt each other. We won't suffer together. See, one day Jesus will make such a difference in our lives and in our relationship that things will be perfect.

Men, remember this. The difference maker in your marriage isn't you, it's Jesus. Jesus's presence is what changes everything, not your presence. Your exciting calling is to date your wife, to love your wife, to help your wife become her future glory-self—to help her become the woman she will one day be on the other side of the grave. But your job is not to be your wife's savior. Your wife needs only one Savior. Your wife needs only one Jesus.

You be you. And let Jesus be Jesus.

Date your wife. And let Jesus save your wife.

The point of your marriage isn't you. The point of your marriage isn't your wife. The point of your marriage is to date your wife in such a way that showcases Jesus and his power to a world of husbands and wives, men and women, boys and girls, in desperate need of a God who can rescue, reconcile, restore, and redeem their broken lives.[4] Marriage isn't ultimate. God is ultimate.

God created marriage so that we could better know and enjoy him. As we date our wives, as we experience the good, the bad, and the new in our marriages—the cycle of failure and grace and growth—we get to know what God is like. Marriage becomes a place where God shows up. We get to know a God who loved us, lost us, and fought to get us back. The point of marriage is the point of life: to know, enjoy, glorify, and experience our triune God.

Men, we have a big mission on our hands. This is bigger than us and bigger than our marriages. This is as big as God. As you date your wife in a world full of broken vows and broken dreams, you spread the news about the God who makes, and keeps, everlasting vows with undeserving people.

There is no "until death do us part" with Jesus. He will never part from us. His vows to his spouse last forever. One day we'll meet the One who can be and do what we could never be and do.

> Then I saw a new heaven and a new earth, for the first heaven and the first earth had passed away, and the sea was no more. And I saw the holy city, new Jerusalem, coming down out of heaven from God, prepared as a bride adorned for her husband. And I heard a loud voice from the throne saying, "Behold, the dwelling place of God is with man. He will dwell with them, and they will be his people, and God himself will be with them as their God. He will wipe away every tear from their eyes, and death shall be

no more, neither shall there be mourning, nor crying, nor pain anymore, for the former things have passed away."

And he who was seated on the throne said, "Behold, I am making all things new." (Rev. 21:1–5)

Men, until then, date your wife.

TAKE ACTION

1. Write out what you'd want your wife to say about you and your pursuit of her if you were to die in the next few years. This is the man you hope to become. Realize that because of Jesus you have the resources to grow into this man. Move forward into the new territory God is calling you.
2. If this book has helped you and your marriage, contact me through my website, www.JustinBuzzard.net, and tell me about it. I'd love to hear your story.
3. Spread the word about *Date Your Wife*. Tell other men and women (married and single) to read this book.

AFTERWORD

To all the dream girls,

That's what we are. We, the wives of the men reading this book (and the future wives of the single men reading this book), are the dream girls. That's why our husbands married us.

As time goes on, as marriages hit year six, seventeen, thirty-one, the dream girl often gets hidden away under layers of stress, bitterness, miscommunication, and selfishness. I'd like to use this opportunity to encourage and advise all of the dream girls out there. This book has been about men stepping up and pursuing their dream girls. But that doesn't mean we are off the hook. We have stepping up and pursuing to do as well.

First of all, remember that God loves marriage. He delights in thriving, intimate marriages. Pray that God would infuse your marriage with new life. Don't waste your time and energies trying to be the perfect woman—I've tried this strategy, and it left me fried and discouraged. You don't have to be a perfect woman. You can't be a perfect woman. Jesus lived a life of perfection in your place. Don't exhaust yourself with striving; rather, rest in Jesus and his perfection. If you are a Christian woman, you are clothed in the righteousness of Jesus and should never strive to be the dream girl in your own strength. Tap into the power of Jesus, as he alone is able to protect and revive your marriage.

After acknowledging that Jesus is your power source, I have four simple suggestions for how to bring your marriage to the next level:

1. Be datable.

Before the wedding band was slipped on our fingers, we made an effort to look good, to smell good, to be sweet. Continue looking good, smelling good, and being sweet throughout the course of your marriage.

2. Respect and encourage your husband.

Use your tongue to encourage him rather than cut him down. Speak highly of him, in public just as much as in private.

3. Spend daily time together.

The "Date-Your-Wife Ground War Sample Schedule" might surprise you. There are lots of one-hour pockets of time together. This is absolutely essential. As children come and life gets busier, many couples become like ships passing in the night. You take turns going out at night, you take turns going on weekends away with friends, you get buried in separate evening projects at home, and before you know it, you are roommates at best. Prioritize one-on-one time with your husband. Write it into the schedule. He will turn into your best friend as you begin to do this.

4. Enjoy frequent sex.

The average woman doesn't need as much sex as the average man, therefore we must go out of our way to make sure that his sex tank is full. It is dangerous to send him into the world with a tank lingering around empty. Take it upon yourself to pursue him. The good news is that it's much easier than we think! Walk down the hall in lingerie and high heels, and your job is pretty much accomplished. If it helps to have a number in your head, we have found that it works best for us to enjoy sex about four times a week. But that is between you and your man.

I pray that this book helps to enrich your marriage. Have faith that God can do great things in and through your marriage! Since Justin's and my engagement, I have regularly prayed, "Jesus, make our marriage a living example of the gift that you intended marriage to be." As we do life in a postmarriage, divorce-ridden world, I invite you to pray this prayer for your marriage as well. And remember, you are the dream girl!

Taylor Buzzard

APPENDIX 1
DATE YOUR WIFE:
ONE HUNDRED IDEAS

Men, you need to come up with your own ideas for how to date your wife. You know your wife better than anyone else. Only you know how to best cultivate and guard the woman God has given you. But sometimes it helps to build off other people's ideas in order to form your own. Here are one hundred Date-Your-Wife ideas to jump-start your own thinking. My prayer is that the power of the gospel would drive how you date your wife and implement these ideas. I came up with the first ninety of these ideas, and readers of my website (www.JustinBuzzard. net) submitted the final ten.

1. Circle the "Take Action" points at the end of each chapter that excite you the most and do them again. My wife likes the four action points at the end of chapter 3.
2. Take your wife out to dinner and tell her how this book has changed you.
3. Spend an evening working on your kiss. Learn how to kiss your wife all over again.
4. Devote an evening a week for the next nine weeks to reading and discussing with your wife *The Meaning of Marriage: Facing the Complexities of Commitment with the Wisdom of God* by Timothy and Kathy Keller (Dutton, 2011).

5. Cut something from your budget and use that money to date your wife.

6. Cut something from your schedule and use that time to date your wife.

7. Schedule a weekend to watch the kids and send your wife off for a personal retreat.

8. Try sleeping naked together.

9. Find a married couple whose marriage is struggling. Adopt them for five months. Take them on double dates once a month for the next five months and coach them toward a healthier marriage. This will help your own marriage more than you can imagine.

10. After your next marriage fight, don't make up—make out. See if making out takes care of the making up.

11. Pray for your wife. Pray for her every day.

12. Attend a wedding. Sit in the back row and spend the whole time whispering memories from your own wedding.

13. Remind your wife of the gospel.

14. Tell your wife the reasons why she is your best friend. Then, talk to your wife about one area of your friendship you want to work on and develop.

15. Make a list of ten things your wife loves to do. Each new time you take your wife on a date, do one of those ten things as your date.

16. Take up a new hobby with your wife; do something new that you're both excited about.

17. Exercise with your wife. Sweat together.

18. Tell your wife that she looks beautiful, and teach your kids to do the same.

19. Spend an evening making love to your wife and reading the Song of Solomon together.

20. Make sure you and your wife are in community and on mission with a healthy, gospel-preaching church.

21. Do the classic date: dinner and a show. Take your wife to dinner and to a movie she wants to watch.

22. Dance with your wife. Use your living room, your backyard, or go to a club.
23. Search your local newspapers for free date ideas: concerts in the park, jazz nights at local clubs, etc.
24. Make your wife laugh. Get good at saying and doing things that cause your wife to laugh.
25. Ask your wife these questions on a regular basis: How are you—how do you feel? What's going on with you and Jesus lately? How can I better love you and our family? How can I pray for you? Are there any adjustments we need to make?
26. Ask your wife to regularly ask you the same type of questions listed above.
27. Tickle your wife.
28. Take a twelve-month honeymoon with your wife. Relive your honeymoon by scheduling a twenty-four-hour getaway for every month of this year. Each month go somewhere new with your wife.
29. Criticize your wife less. Compliment your wife more.
30. Devote one hour each night for alone time with your wife. Talk about how your days went. Joke around with each other. Cultivate your friendship. Talk honestly about what's going on in your lives. Help each other. Encourage each other. Pray together.
31. Mark your wife's birthday, your wedding anniversary, and Mother's Day on your calendar every year and plan to make those days special.
32. Talk to your wife about her friendships. Ask her how things are going with her girlfriends. Pray for her friendships.
33. Worship God with your wife.
34. Make dinner for your wife.
35. Think about something your wife never had as a girl and give that to her.
36. Ask your wife to read *Date Your Wife* and tell you what she liked about it.
37. Write a love note to your wife. Tell her all over again what she means to you.

38. Give your wife a massage.

39. Give your wife an orgasm (that's a whole 'nother book).

40. Do something with your wife that both of you are scared to do.

41. Tuck your wife in to bed. Kiss her. Pray over her. Stroke her hair as she falls asleep.

42. Spend an evening stargazing with your wife and talking about dreams you have for the future.

43. Spend an evening reminiscing with your wife about all you've been through together and all God has done and redeemed in your life together.

44. Invite your wife to work. Ask her to come visit you at work so that she can see your world and better understand what you're facing every day.

45. Compliment your wife on her inner beauty.

46. Compliment your wife on her outer beauty.

47. Enter a contest or competition with your wife: a running race, a pie-baking competition, a dance contest, etc. Do something with your wife where you compete against others.

48. Serve your wife breakfast in bed.

49. Devote the next month to studying a book of the Bible with your wife. Take twenty minutes several nights a week to read, discuss, and pray through a shorter book such as Ephesians or Philippians.

50. Visit your roots. Visit where your wife grew up and where you grew up. Learn more about each other's backgrounds.

51. Tell your wife how much you rely on her and need her. Tell her how much it means to you when she pursues you.

52. Pray with your wife.

53. Lose a marriage fight. Let your wife win.

54. Tell your wife what's going on inside you—what you're afraid of, what you're excited about, and what you need help with.

55. Draw a bubble bath for your wife and tell her to stop what she's doing and hop in. Depending on her mood, hop in with her.

56. Surprise your wife by cleaning the house while she is out running errands.

57. Make your wife a handmade gift of some sort.

58. Watch your wife closely this week and compile a list of admirable attributes that your wife exhibits. At the end of the week share the list with your wife, telling her how much you appreciate who she is and who she's becoming.

59. Hold your wife's hand often, in public and in private.

60. Tell your wife that you love her.

61. Tell your wife that Jesus loves her more than you do.

62. Set a weekly date night. Each week rotate going out and staying in for your date night.

63. Spend an evening naked together while doing a Bible study of Proverbs 5:18–19, "Let your fountain be blessed, and rejoice in the wife of your youth, a lovely deer, a graceful doe. Let her breasts fill you at all times with delight; be intoxicated always in her love."[1]

64. Assign a day of "bed rest" to your wife. Make her take a day to rest, relax, and not accomplish anything productive.

65. Pick a TV show you and your wife both like and watch it together every week.

66. Get into wine together. If you and your wife both drink alcohol, start learning about wine together. Try out different wines every week and learn what kind of wines you both like to drink.

67. Surprise your wife by ordering her a subscription to a magazine she really likes.

68. Ask your wife to speak to you in French and kiss you in French.[2]

69. Call your wife in the middle of the day just to say, "I love you."

70. Give your wife a foot massage.

71. Read through your old junior high and high school yearbooks together.

72. Cancel work for the day and do something special with your wife.

73. Watch the kids and send your wife out to a local coffee shop to enjoy an hour or two alone.

74. Take dancing lessons with your wife.

75. Invite some married couples over to your house for an evening and, together with your wife, talk with them about the importance of dating your wife. Attempt to start a Date-Your-Wife movement in your neighborhood/circle of friends/church.

76. Tell your wife you're sorry.

77. Detect the one thing you do that most annoys your wife and stop doing it.

78. Have a photographer take new pictures of you and your wife. Put these pictures up in your home.

79. Shower with your wife.

80. Train your kids to say sweet things to your wife. (I've taught our boys to regularly say to their mom, "Mom, you are beautiful and godly.")

81. Study your wife. Get to know your wife and how she ticks; there's always more to learn.[3]

82. Remember things that are important to your wife.

83. Vacation with your wife without your kids, without your work, and without your cell phone and computer.

84. Ask your wife about her day. Tell her about your day. Do this every day.

85. Prepare a basin of soapy water and wash your wife's feet.[4]

86. Cuddle your wife.

87. Revisit the scene of your wedding, thank God for your marriage, and pray through your wedding vows. Then go drink some champagne or eat cake.

88. Brag about your wife in front of other people.

89. Get in better shape; take better care of yourself and how you look for the sake of your wife—lose some weight, get a haircut, throw out those old clothes you've been wearing since college, buy some clothes that you actually look good in, shave, etc.

90. Notice when your wife is particularly tired, drained, or

stressed out. On such days step in and take one or two responsibilities off your wife's plate.

91. Watch the kids and send your wife out for a pedicure. —Jeff Slavich (57), San Jose.

92. Invite your wife's best friends over and cook dinner for your wife and her friends. —Mez McConnell (38), Edinburgh.

93. Keep fresh dry erase markers in the bathroom. Periodically write your wife an encouraging note on the bathroom mirror that she'll read when she wakes up. —Seth Hoffman (26), Portsmouth.

94. Eat apart from your kids occasionally. Let the kids eat pasta at a kids' table while you dine by candlelight with your wife in the adjoining room. —Sandy Grant (42), Wollongong, Australia.

95. Give your wife a mini-vacation every Saturday morning. Watch the kids while your wife takes Saturday morning by herself to recharge. —Jeff Kaldahl (33), San Antonio.

96. Write in a greeting card the top five reasons you chose your wife as your bride. Take your wife out to dinner at her favorite restaurant and go over these top five reasons, one by one, while looking in her eyes. Give her the card to keep afterward. —Joan Buzzard (58), Sacramento.

97. Pray with your wife. Play with your wife. Plan with your wife. Pursue your wife. Do this every day. —Ian Hagerman (28), San Jose.

98. Create a photo album with your wife of some of your most cherished memories together. —Tina Jung (26), El Cerrito, CA.

99. Go on an outdoor adventure with your wife—do something neither of you have ever done before. —Colin Dobrin (28), Newport Beach.

100. Create a choose-your-adventure date night with three stages. For each stage present your wife with two options. For example, Stage 1: manicure or massage; Stage 2: restaurant A or restaurant B; Stage 3: dessert or after-dinner drinks. —Danny Slavich (30), Hollywood.

APPENDIX 2
DATE YOUR WIFE:
A MESSAGE FROM A
NINETY-YEAR-OLD HUSBAND

Men, I've got great news for you! Take it from a ninety-year-old husband who, for the past three years, has had the privilege of serving as caregiver for his wife, and is now in the twilight period of life here below. Five years ago we were running around like a couple of newlyweds. Then suddenly my wife, Jean, began to fail. Her health rapidly declined. We brought in help, but soon Jean had to move from our apartment into the nursing wing of the retirement complex.

"But," you ask, "what kind of a privilege is that?" The privilege is the incredible opportunity of loving your wife better than ever before as you move through life. I used to think I loved Jean, and I did. I made the living, helped a bit with the kids, planned vacations, and tried to stay upbeat. What I didn't find out until these last few years is the remarkable personal growth that comes from giving yourself for the benefit of another. I wouldn't trade the last three years for anything in the world.

We've been married for sixty years. Did you know that

marriage has a way of getting better the longer it goes? These last three years of marriage have been the best of all.

Someone defined love as "placing the welfare of the other ahead of your own." That's the kind of love that pays great dividends. Careful now: you don't love for what you get out of it. What happens is that genuine love—a life invested in another—simply works out that way. No wonder, because in all three Synoptic Gospels Jesus says, "The one who tries to save his life will certainly lose it; but the one who loses his life will be rewarded with a full and abundant life."[1]

There is no question that the more you love (put first) your wife, the richer and more rewarding your own life will be. I call that good news all around. And life is full of opportunities to carry out this challenge. Don't forget to keep dating your wife. It may seem like a trifle, but little acts of selfless concern communicate far more effectively than almost anything else. Your wife's welfare is in your hands. Provide real leadership, not the bossy kind, but gentle illustrations of the fact that her well-being—physical, emotional, and spiritual—is a major concern in your life.

Invest wisely! Take Jesus at his word. I am ninety years old. Nine decades have proven to me that God's kind of love heals, encourages, and directs with unfailing accuracy.

Men, the message is: Lay down your life for your wife; lose your life and you will save it!

Dr. Bob Mounce

P.S. Please watch this two-minute video that shows how I date my wife: www.justinbuzzard.net/2011/12/04/date-your-wife-when-your-90-years-old

NOTES

Acknowledgments

1. Charles Spurgeon quoted in Larry J. Michael, *Spurgeon on Leadership: Key Insights for Christian Leaders from the Prince of Preachers* (Grand Rapids, MI: Kregel, 2010), 131.

Preface: Why You ~~Should Read~~ Want to Read This Book

1. I guess you could say that I wrote this book because I was ticked off. I was ticked off about the condition of men and marriages, so I wrote a book to make better men and better marriages.

Chapter 2: Who Invented Marriage, and Why?

1. Cru is also named after Cru Jones, a young man who overcame obstacles to achieve his dream to win Helltrack, a BMX race, in the 1986 film, *Rad* (TriStar Pictures). It was my favorite movie as a kid. My middle son, Hudson, is named after Hudson Taylor, a missionary to China known for his great bravery and faith. My youngest son, Gus (full name Augustine), is named after Saint Augustine, a fourth-century theologian who changed the world and penned a quote that's significantly shaped my life and thinking: "Love God and do as you please."

2. I believe the Bible clearly teaches that Adam and Eve were real, historical people specially created by God. The New Testament repeatedly argues for the historicity of the first husband and wife:
- Jesus refers to the creation of Adam and Eve as real, historical events (Matt. 19:4–6; Mark 10:6).
- Luke attributes a father to everyone in his genealogy except for Adam, calling Adam "the son of God" (Luke 3:38).
- Paul declares to the Greeks in Athens, "And he made from one man every nation of mankind to live on all the face of the earth" (Acts 17:26).
- Paul refers to the sin of "one man . . . the transgression of Adam, who was a type of the one who was to come" (Rom. 5:12–14) and

refs to the historical Jesus with the same language: "For if many died through one man's trespass, much more have the grace of God and the free gift by the grace of that one man Jesus Christ abounded for many" (Rom. 5:15).

- Paul addresses Eve's unique creation, "For man was not made from woman, but woman from man" (1 Cor. 11:8); "For Adam was formed first, then Eve" (1 Tim. 2:13).
- Paul speaks of Adam as a real person, again comparing him with Jesus: "For as in Adam all die, so also in Christ shall all be made alive" (1 Cor. 15:22).

3. I've been teaching my four-year-old and two-year-old sons how to prepare for marriage. If you bump into them, ask them this question: "What do you have to do to get married?" They will then recite to you: "1) Love Jesus; 2) Get a job; 3) Pick a girl who loves Jesus."

4. After one year of marriage Martin Luther wrote this in a letter to a friend. "Katharina von Bora," Reformation Tours, accessed July 13, 2011, http://www.reformationtours.com/site/490868/page/204052.

Chapter 3: Where Marriages Go Wrong, Part I: The Husband

1. E-mail message to author, March 11, 2011.

2. Show me a couple with an unhealthy sex life, and I'll show you a couple with an unhealthy marriage. Sex is a key measurement in your marriage. Sex forces you to deal with the hurt, sin, and problems in your relationship. From my experience, married couples who have an active and healthy sex life have a healthy marriage.

3. Most people miss the fact that a thriving sex life is an act of spiritual warfare. This is what Paul teaches when he addresses married couples, sex, and temptation in 1 Corinthians 7:5: "Do not deprive one another, except perhaps by agreement for a limited time, that you may devote yourselves to prayer; but then come together again, so that Satan may not tempt you because of your lack of self-control."

4. E-mail message from Taylor Buzzard, March 12, 2011.

5. Marriage is where the real dating begins. Single guys don't know how to date; they only know how to sell themselves. "Dating" is a relatively recent phenomenon. Around the turn of the century modern "dating" developed, the word first appearing in print in 1914. See a discussion on the history of dating in Timothy and Kathy Keller, *The Meaning of*

Marriage: Facing the Complexities of Commitment with the Wisdom of God (New York: Dutton, 2011), 204–207. As I argued in this chapter, I define dating on the basis of Genesis 2:15, not on the basis of our culture. I suppose if I had written this book in the eighteenth century I would've titled it: *Court Your Wife: Why Courtship Should Never Stop*. Had I written it in the first century I would've titled it, *Enjoy Your Wife: Making the Best of Your Arranged Marriage*.

Chapter 4: Where Marriages Go Wrong, Part II: The Husband's Religion

1. Today this marriage is thriving. Deep reconciliation and healing has taken place and my friend and his wife couldn't be happier.

Chapter 6: Where Marriages Go Right, Part I: The Husband

1. For there to be new life, there must be death. For there to be resurrection, there must be a crucifixion. Men, when God seems to be killing you, he might actually be saving you. God humbles us and puts to death areas and arenas of our life in order to set us free and make us into the men he's called us to be. Don't fear the death; it leads to new life.

2. Simon and Garfunkel, "I Am a Rock," *Sounds of Silence* (New York: Columbia, 1966) 33⅓ rpm.

3. The excuse most common among men is a "woundedness" excuse. Men excuse their sin and poor treatment of their wife because of ways they've been wounded by their wife, by others, or by their past. As long as the victim card is played, men stay stuck and marriages stay stuck. The woundedness excuse is as unmanly as it gets; it's using someone else's sin to excuse your own sin. Excuses are actually a form of slavery—letting what someone else did to you control your behavior.

Chapter 7: Where Marriages Go Right, Part II: The Husband's Gospel

1. The pressures and pleasures of marriage have the power to mature you like no other human relationship or experience. Marriage brings out the worst in you and the best in you, and in the process, radically changes you.

2. Ray Ortlund attributes this quote to Tim Keller, Mars Hill Lectures and Seminars http://ballard.marshill.com/2011/02/15/marriage-family-seminar/.

Chapter 8: Where Marriages Go Right, *Part III: The Husband's Action*

1. This depiction of the American story is taken from *The Storyformed Way,* week 1, slides, a curriculum developed by Soma Communities: www.somacommunities.org. The curriculum can be accessed here: http://www.gcmcollective.com/article/story-formed-way/.

2. Forgetting isn't so much the issue; remembrance is the issue. Forgiveness isn't a matter of how we forget, but of how we remember.

3. Men, a lot of you are looking at pornography and other women. Stop it. If this is going on in your marriage, repent of this in front of God and in front of your wife. Decide that pornography will no longer be part of your life and ask God for the grace and power to keep this commitment. Get help from other men who will help lead you toward gospel-driven change in this area of your life.

4. It's significant that Scripture's most important treatment on spiritual warfare (Ephesians 6) comes immediately after Scripture's most important treatment on marriage (Ephesians 5).

Chapter 9: A New Dream for Your Marriage

1. These are not their real names; my friends wanted their names disguised because they were embarrassed that I was making such a big deal about their marriage.

Chapter 10: How to Date Your Wife: Develop the Air War

1. Men, make it your goal to be famous at home. I want to be famous at home, taking great care of my wife and kids. Care less about the fame of men. Be famous at home.

2. Go to my website, www.JustinBuzzard.net, for more details about the Date-Your-Wife Plan, other *Date Your Wife* materials, and speaking requests.

3. The costs cited in this plan are real. If you do some creative, strategic thinking and hunt for deals and promotions, you can execute a plan like this with a tight budget.

Chapter 11: How to Date Your Wife: Develop the Ground War

1. For over six years now we have protected sundown Friday to sundown Saturday as a family Sabbath. This gives rhythm to our week and we can't imagine life without it.

2. Spending a few hours alone together isn't really a planned thing in our marriage. Taylor and I just love being together, so by default most every night of the week we hang out on the couch or in the backyard together. A sign of a strong marriage and strong friendship is that you genuinely enjoy each other's company. The secret to this is, of course, gospel love. My wife knows the worst about me, yet she loves me and will not leave me. Such security is an incredible basis for friendship. This is why divorce is so painful—it's knowing the worst about someone and deciding not to love and not to stay.

Chapter 12: Date Your Wife until Death Do You Part

1. I learned the phrase "future glory-self" from Tim Keller's sermon series on marriage, a series that Taylor and I listened to several years ago. That sermon series has now been expanded into an excellent book, *The Meaning of Marriage: Facing the Complexities of Commitment with the Wisdom of God* (New York: Dutton, 2011). Keller's discussion of our "future glory-selves" can be found on page 120.

2. On September 18, 2011, I planted a church in Silicon Valley that I named "Garden City Church." The name has a double meaning. When San Jose (the first city in California) was founded in 1777, people often referred to the city as the "Garden City" because everything they planted grew and flourished in the city's good soil and temperate climate. This was a prophetic name for the city that's grown to become the "Capital of Silicon Valley" and America's tenth-largest city. The other influence for the name came from the Bible, as the story of the Bible starts in a garden (Genesis 1–2) and ends in a garden city (Revelation 21–22). San Jose still has a few institutions that carry the old name of the city—a casino, a liquor store, and a sanitation business. My hope is that Garden City Church brings new flourishing to this great city. Learn more at www.gardencitysanjose.com.

3. I know Matthew 22:30 says, "For in the resurrection they neither marry nor are given in marriage, but are like angels in heaven," but I don't think it's wise to construct an entire postresurrection, antimarriage

theology from this one verse. Whatever marriage relationships look like in heaven, they will be something better than what they are right now.

4. Our vision for our marriage, something that Taylor and I pray about and hope for, is that it proclaims the gospel to others.

Appendix 1: Date Your Wife: One Hundred Ideas

1. My wife tells me I have the hormones of a sixteen-year-old boy. I tell her that deep down, all men do.

2. Taylor majored in French in college.

3. The most important insight I've gained from studying my wife this past year: Taylor gets really turned on when I do the dishes. This is important information! I now do the dishes a lot more often. Men and women are different. My wife gets turned on when I do housework; I get turned on when she takes her clothes off.

4. When I proposed to Taylor at that mossy log in the redwood forest, earlier in the day I had hidden a bucket of water behind the log. After asking her to marry me and giving her a ring, I stayed down on my knees and washed her feet to symbolize the servant leadership of Jesus and to communicate the type of leader I wanted to be in our marriage. Service is probably the thing I'm the worst at in our marriage, but I'm growing.

Appendix 2: Date Your Wife: A Message from a Ninety-Year-Old Husband

1. This paraphrase of Matt. 16:25; Mark 8:35; Luke 9:24 is from my book *Jesus, In His Own Words* (Nashville, TN: Broadman, 2010), 117.

GENERAL INDEX

SCRIPTURE INDEX

Personal Notes

Personal Notes

Personal Notes

Personal Notes

Personal Notes

Personal Notes

Personal Notes

Personal Notes

Personal Notes